# The Board Game Designer's Guide to Getting Published

Making a great board game and pitching it to publishers are two completely different things.

If you've got a game that you want to share with the world but don't know what to do next, this book will help you navigate through exactly what steps to take.

You'll discover:

- How to find the right publisher
- Exactly what publishers are looking for
- How to create a sell sheet that will actually sell your game
- How to negotiate the best deal and get paid more for your game
- What to look out for in contracts to make sure you don't get exploited

You'll learn from Joe's experiences as a full-time board game designer and instructor, along with tips and stories from a dozen other published designers, plus the exact things that publishers want. Direct from 16 established publishers.

# THE BOARD GAME DESIGN COURSE

Make sure to go to tinyurl.com/bgbonuspage to download all the bonuses and goodies mentioned in the book, including the 10 Minute Board Game Blueprint, sell sheet examples, pitch and email templates, the video that landed my first published game, plus a whole lot more.

# The Board Game Designer's Guide to Getting Published

## How to Find the Right Publisher, Know What to Look for in a Contract, and Get Your Board Game Signed

Joe Slack

CRC Press is an imprint of the
Taylor & Francis Group, an informa business

First edition published 2023
by CRC Press
6000 Broken Sound Parkway NW, Suite 300, Boca Raton, FL 33487-2742

and by CRC Press
4 Park Square, Milton Park, Abingdon, Oxon, OX14 4RN

*CRC Press is an imprint of Taylor & Francis Group, LLC*



**Library of Congress Cataloging-in-Publication Data**

Names: Slack, Joe, author.
Title: The board game designer's guide to getting published: how to find the right publisher, know what to look for in a contract, and get your board game signed/Joe Slack.
Description: Boca Raton, FL: Taylor and Francis, 2022. | Includes bibliographical references and index.
Identifiers: LCCN 2022023869 (print) | LCCN 2022023870 (ebook) |
ISBN 9781032369891 (hardback) | ISBN 9781032369884 (paperback) |
ISBN 9781003334828 (ebook)
Subjects: LCSH: Board games–Publishing–Handbooks, manuals, etc.
Classification: LCC GV1312. S527 2022 (print) | LCC GV1312 (ebook) |
DDC 794–dc23/eng/20220630
LC record available at https://lccn.loc.gov/2022023869
LC ebook record available at https://lccn.loc.gov/2022023870

ISBN: 978-1-032-36989-1 (hbk)
ISBN: 978-1-032-36988-4 (pbk)
ISBN: 978-1-003-33482-8 (ebk)

DOI: 10.1201/9781003334828

Typeset in Garamond
by KnowledgeWorks Global Ltd.

*To my wonderful, amazingly supportive wife, Lisa, and son, Evan.*
*I couldn't do this without you.*

# Contents

## Section II
## Everything You Need before You Pitch to Publishers



## Section III
## How to Find the Right Publisher

## Section VI
## Contracts—Understanding What's Important to You



## Section VII
## Stories from the Battlefield

# Acknowledgments

This book wouldn't be nearly as comprehensive without the contributions of numerous other game designers and publishers who were kind enough to answer my questions and share their advice.

First, thank you to the many helpful game designers who shared their stories and amazing advice—Elizabeth Hargrave, Chris Chung, Scott Rogers, Emerson Matsuuchi, Eric Slauson, Adrian Ademescu, Asger Harding Granerud, Don Eskridge, Seiji Kanai, Phil Walker-Harding, Gordon Hamilton, and Alexander Pfister.

Next, thank you to the amazing publishers for contributing invaluable insights into what a designer needs to do to pitch his/her game successfully—Cody Thompson at Gold Nugget Games, Paul Saxberg at Roxley Game Laboratory, Adam McCrimmon at XYZ Game Labs, Helaina Cappel at KTBG/Burnt Island Games, Daniel Kazmaier at Steeped Games, Joshua Lobkowicz at Grey Fox Games, Filip Milunski at Lucky Duck Games, Justin DeWitt at Fireside Games, Jason Schneider at Gamewright, Richard MacRae at Analog Game Studios, Curt Covert at Smirk & Dagger, Seth Jaffee at Tasty Minstrel Games, Carla Kopp at Weird Giraffe Games, Jamey Stegmaier at Stonemaier Games, Nick Bentley at North Star Games, and Julia Patrick at Chronicle Books.

To all the amazing game designers and community members I've learned from, and in many cases became friends with, over the years, I couldn't have done this without learning from all of you. Thank you, Sylvain Plante, Gabe Barrett, Nazareno Properzi, Daryl Andrews, Jonathan Gilmour, Rob Daviau, Steve Jackson, Matt Leacock, Sen-Foong Lim, Jay Cormier, Uwe Rosenberg, Kristian Amundsen Ostby, Wolfgang Warsch, Rudiger Dorn, Kane Klenko, Alan Moon, Bruno Cathala, Kevin Lanzing, JB Howell, Vlaada Chvatil, Tom Vasel, Luke Laurie, Eduardo Baraf, Colby Dauch, Ben Gerber, Gil Hova, Daniel Zayas, the late James Mathe, Artem Safarov, Mark Kolb, Pam Walls, Shannon McDowell, Matthew Hester, Kevin Carmichael,

Allysha Tulk, Peter Hayward, Daniel Rocchi, Jeff Fraser, Stephanie Metcalf, Marek Tupy, Harry Timson, David Van Drunen, David Laciak, Miles Bossons, Andy Kim, Shawn Clouthier, Chris Cormier, Sherri Cormier, AJ Brandon, Sean Calligan, Maryann Buri, Marc Gurwiz, Chris Backe, Graham MacLean, Mikhail Honoridez, Reed Mascola, Jack Kennedy, Al Leduc, Josh Derkson, Brian Stumme, Adam Springer, Francois Valentine, Josh Sprung, Caren Sprung, Kenny Valles, Scott Kelly, Bill Murphy, Erica Bouyouris, Grace Lee, Tristam Rossin, Corey Keller, Chad Crider, Michael Chartrand, Stephen Sauer, Danny Goodisman, Lutfi Nahin, Bryan Dale, Brent Wilde, David Clay Gonsalves, Darryl T Jones, Mark Maia, Brittany Maia, Chris Medeiros, Jesse Anderson, Joel Colombo, Amelie Le-Roche, Patrick Hardy, Adam Leamey, Darrin Lauritzen, Colin Eatock, Jeff Toth, Miles Bossons, Chris Zinsli, and the whole team at XYZ Game Labs.

A special thanks to my editor Rebecca Reid.

A huge thank you to Drew Corkill for all the formatting help and designing a fantastic cover.

Thank you to Andrew Stackhouse for sharing your valuable contract examples.

Thank you, Amine Bo, for the great book title suggestion.

To my incredible friends and family, Jason Deline, Helena Patte, Matthew Guillemette, Margie Guillemette, Aizick Grimann, Lubin Martinez, Lucas Cesarone, Daniel Longmire, Dave Neal, Renee Laviolette, Claudia Mendez, Matt Mitchell, Cory Bildfell, Rob Slack, Kerri Beaulieu, Sawyer Slack, Kenya Slack, Penny Slack, John Acuna, Cindy Alexander, Caitlin Hartley, Jordan Loshinsky, Melissa McCarthy, Kate McDougall, Stu Sackler, Siva Bradshaw, Shannon Boyce, Marco Garcia, Helen Deline, Gary Deline, Paul Brown, Nan Brooks, Jane Goldthorpe, Mike Sone, Adam DeVita, Frances Maxwell, Voula Maroulis, Jeremy Banks, Nathan Frias, Chad Nikolic, Margarita Prunskus, Pat Prunskus, Yvonne Tellis, James Pawelkiewicz, Leah Smith, Adam Smith, Momo MacLeod, Dave Rossi, Belinda Rossi, Krista Miller, Bernard Blassnig, Rob Routh, Kim Routh, Anna Murray, Helen Taylor, Steve Camacho, Andrew Gibson, Kelly Walk Hines, Lana Jo Borgholthaus, Mike Indovina, Shannon Wylie, Kunle Bristow, Deb Piskunov, and Maks Piskunov. Thank you all for your support and for playing so many early prototypes of my games.

Thank you to my parents, Nancy and Bob Slack. Thank you for everything you do and for always being so supportive.

Last but not least, thank you, Lisa and Evan, for being there for me and letting me live my dream!

# About the Author

**Joe Slack** is a healthcare data guru turned full-time board game designer and game design instructor. He has now combined his passions for board game design and helping others into one. That means he works with other board game designers to help them get unstuck and create amazing games they can't wait to share with the world.

Joe is the #1 best-selling author of *The Board Game Designer's Guide, The Board Game Designer's Guide to Getting Published,* and *The Top 10 Mistakes New Board Game Designers Make (and How to Avoid Them).*

Joe has four games published with different publishers (*Zoo Year's Eve, Kingdom's Candy Monsters, Four Word Thinking,* and *King of Indecision*), along with one self-published game, the solo campaign game *Relics of Rajavihara.*

Joe has also taught game design and development at Wilfrid Laurier University (near Toronto, Canada), and currently runs two online game design courses (the Board Game Design Course and the Creation to Publication Program) that he developed himself, along with a membership site for game designers.

Go to www.boardgamedesigncourse.com to check out his blog, resources, books, and courses for game designers. You can also see what games he's currently working on at www.crazylikeabox.com.

# Introduction

In the Board Game Designer's Guide, which was my first book on the topic, I covered a lot of ground and at the time I didn't think there was much more to say. Boy, was I wrong!

Since my book's release, I've spoken to dozens, if not hundreds, of game designers about their challenges, and one that comes up repeatedly is the difficulty of getting their games published. It's one thing to create a great game, but it's another thing entirely to find a great publisher that's the right match for your game, create and deliver a strong pitch, and get your game signed.

They're completely different skill sets.

Someone who's a great game designer may not be good at, or even want to travel to a bunch of conventions and other events to meet with publishers and pitch their game.

Fortunately, there are many ways to reach out to publishers, get their attention, and get your game signed. You don't have to travel, spend tons of time and money going to Cons, or fill out hundreds of game submission forms for publishers that will never contact you.

In fact, each of the first four games I signed with publishers went through completely different routes.

The first game I signed was with a major publisher whom I've still never even met face to face or even spoken with over the phone. What happened was another designer saw a word game that would later be called *Four Word Thinking* that I was co-designing and thought it would be a good fit for the publisher they had just signed a game with. He put us in direct contact with the person in charge of submissions, and this referral led to getting my first game signed.

DOI: 10.1201/9781003334828-1

The next game I signed, which coincidentally happened the very next day, was with a local publisher I developed a friendship with. We met at Breakout Con, where he playtested a couple of my games and he absolutely loved them. We continued to see each other at different local gaming events and became friends. When I showed him my light strategy game, *King of Indecision*, he was immediately taken with it. Shortly after this, he asked for the prototype so that he could evaluate the game. The rest, as they say, is history.

I later challenged myself to create an 18-card game after hearing a podcast with Jason Tagmire from Buttonshy games. I entered this game in the Board Game Design Lab design challenge, a contest for members, and although it didn't make it past the first round, one of the judges was a publisher who really liked the game. He asked if I would show it to him at Origins Game Fair, which I had mentioned I would be attending. We played the game there and his team immediately asked for the prototype. Shortly after that, I had my third game signed. It's called *Zoo Year's Eve* and it has been published by XYZ Game Labs.

My fourth game signing was a bit more unusual. I had another game designer contact me out of the blue and ask if I was interested in co-designing a game that was inspired by *World of Warcraft*. After some discussion, we agreed to work on the game together. However, it was a big undertaking and we knew it would take some time. In the meantime, he had another game called *Kingdom's Candy: Monsters* that was in development and asked if I would do some playtesting for him. I was glad to help. Not only did I run a few playtests over the next couple of weeks, but I also made several rule revisions. He was so impressed with how much work I had put into the game and the improvements I had suggested that he asked for my help co-designing this game as well. *Kingdom's Candy: Monsters* has since been funded successfully on Kickstarter, reaching 168% of the funding goal.

I've also had some success pitching games at meetings, at vendor booths, and speed dating events. These have often resulted in publishers taking a prototype for evaluation, or at the very least, the start of a good relationship. Some have resulted in a pass, others have suggested more development work, and some games are currently being evaluated.

Now, I want to emphasize that this book is all about how to pitch and get your game signed by a publisher. Although I do mention Kickstarter and self-publishing, that is not the focus of this book. If you're interested in learning more about self-publishing and crowdfunding, I would highly recommend Jamey Stegmaier's excellent book, *A Crowdfunder's Strategy Guide* (tinyurl.com/crowdguide), and his *Kickstarter Lessons blog* (tinyurl.com/kslessons).

It's also important to keep in mind that although you may find the right publisher, create a killer sell sheet, and have your pitch down cold, none of these will matter if your game isn't great. It's no longer enough to have just a good game. It has to really stand out. As the expression goes, you can put lipstick on a pig, but it's still a pig.

So, in the first section we're going to go through what it takes to make sure your game is great before you set out to pitch it to a publisher. This will increase your chances of success greatly.

Following this, I'll help you put together everything you need to pitch your game effectively, show you how to get your game in front of the right publisher (including methods that don't require traveling to tons of events), how to seal the deal, and what to look for (and what dangers to avoid) in contracts.

So, without further ado, let's finish making your game even better and get it signed so that you can finally become a published game designer!

# Section I

# What You Need to Do before You Even Think of Pitching Your Game

# 1

# Making a Great Game

> With the volume of games being released, there is very little room for "good" games anymore. They have to be "great."
>
> **– Justin DeWitt, Fireside Games**

Sure, you want your game published. Who wouldn't?

But here's a question you may not have asked yourself: Is my game publishable?

## Is Your Game Good Enough?

Trying to get your game signed is very much like looking for a job. Let's say you find a job that has great pay, good benefits, and is within a well-respected company with lots of growth opportunities. You'd absolutely love to get the position.

Unfortunately, you're not the one to choose whether you get the job. That's up to the employer. They must narrow down the field of candidates from all the applications they receive. Then, they will only interview those whom they feel are the best match. This will come down to the candidate's education, experience, and if they would be a good fit for the company and culture.

Similarly, as a game designer, it's important to look at both sides of the equation.

It's critical to understand what the vision is for your game so you can bring this out as strongly as possible, as well as recognize what publishers are looking for, and to pitch your game effectively.

Let's dive in.

DOI: 10.1201/9781003334828-3

## Develop a Vision for Your Game

When you come up with the idea for a game, it's important to develop and truly understand what your vision is for this game. Ask yourself what kind of experience you want players to have.

Although the theme, mechanics, end condition, restrictions, and components could change dramatically, your vision for the game is the one thing that should remain constant.

Do you want your game to evoke stories and memories that people will always remember?

Is tension what you're aiming for?

Perhaps you want players to feel a sense of brilliance or accomplishment.

Whatever your vision is, you want to make sure that players are consistently having the type of experience that you're aiming for.

## Work Out Any Rough Spots

Once your game is accomplishing your vision and players are really enjoying the experience you've created, you'll want to make sure the game plays as smoothly as possible.

Are there any rare instances where something strange happens or a problem occurs? These are known as edge cases. You'll want to get these ironed out, as you don't want to have a lot of exceptions or rules required for those infrequent things occurring.

Keep your rules clear and straightforward. Every time a player must refer back to the rulebook, they are taken away from the game, and the flow is disrupted. If this happens multiple times, players may become disengaged and lose interest in your game, which is the opposite of what you want.

So, playtest your game a lot, with plenty of different people. Identify and remove as many little exceptions as possible. Your aim is to get your game to flow smoothly to keep players engaged throughout.

## Players Should Be Asking You This …

Here's a question that I hear all the time: How do you know when your game is done?

It's a tricky question to answer, as it is more based on feeling than anything scientific. Some designers even joke that your game is done when you're tired of it and never want to play it again. Others say no games are ever finished, they just get published.

If you feel like you've taken your game as far as you possibly can, this may be an indication that you're getting close. It may be time to hand it over to a game developer to finish the job, whether it is you contracting this out if you are self-publishing, or for your publisher's developer or development team to help get your game across the finish line.

I always find that the best indication that my game is ready to pitch to publishers is that players are consistently asking to play my game again, or even better, they are asking if they can buy a copy. If you have many people wanting to buy your prototype, which isn't even a finished product yet, you know you're onto something!

## Take Action

I want you to **write down the vision for your game**—what you want players to experience. Along with the vision, document all the other aspects of your game, including the theme, mechanics, and victory conditions. Note that all these other aspects may change as you iterate and improve upon your game, but your vision should remain untouched.

I've put together an easy-to-complete blueprint to help you document all this information quickly and so you will have it available in one convenient place.

Go to tinyurl.com/bgbonuspage to download the 10 Minute Board Game Blueprint, as well as access tons of other great goodies.

# 2

# Understanding What Makes Your Game Unique (and the Hook)

> To be honest, there needs to be a specific hook that really sets the game apart in today's market.
>
> **–Dan Kazmaier, Steeped Games**

Your game can't just be a copy of an existing game. There must be something that sets it apart.

Yet, being too unique can pose other problems as well.

Let's look at how to make your game unique without making it so different that no one will play it.

## Discovering What Makes Your Game Unique

With thousands of games being released each year (at Cons, on Kickstarter, in retail), there's a lot of competition. Your game needs to stand out.

So, think about what people love about your game. What do they talk about that intrigues them so much? What makes your game different than all the others?

Your game can't be just like another game with a different theme or one minor change. Is it just another deckbuilder? Another dexterity game like all the rest?

It's a crowded market. Your game must be something different. It must *do* something different.

This is often referred to as "the hook". What is it that hooks people in and makes them want to play your game, even though they know nothing about it?

DOI: 10.1201/9781003334828-4

## Why Familiarity Is So Important

At the same time, while you want your game to be unique, you don't want it to be *too unique.* It's ok for people to compare your game to others, as long as it's not *too similar.*

For example, my game, *King of Indecision* is a bit like *Catan* in some ways. It has hex tiles and involves some trading, but with the market only, not with other players. However, that's where the similarities end. The rest of the gameplay is around point-to-point movement and jockeying for position with other players to be the one who offers the King the most goods just before he changes his mind. So, it's not really like *Catan* at all. But when people see *King of Indecision* on the table, there's something familiar about it.

When people recognize some similarities in your game, it's easier for them to learn and get into your game.

On the other hand, if your game is *too unique*, people may not be able to understand it, and your game may be too difficult to market, etc.

Changes and innovations take place in steps. *Dominion* is considered to be the 1st deckbuilder, and others have since come along and built on this. But without *Dominion*, these other games probably wouldn't have existed.

This applies to many games—*Jenga* had to come before *Junk Art*, *Crokinole* had to come before *Catacombs Cubes*, and *D&D* had to come before other dungeon crawlers and RPGs.

## Evoking Curiosity

You need to ask yourself, "what is it about my game that grabs people's attention?"

Any game that stands out or physically *stands up* makes people stop and watch or want to play. Think about games with 3D elements, games that provide a tactile experience, and games with toy-like elements (such as *Slide Quest*, *Forbidden Sky*, and *Fireball Island*).

Think about your senses and games that limit those senses, such as *Nyctophobia*, *The Mind*, and *Shadows in the Forest*. Players are limited in their communication or vision. These constraints place a restriction on players that makes the game more challenging, but also a more memorable experience.

Ask yourself what you can add to your game that will make people want to stop in their tracks.

Part of making your game unique and attractive is being able to draw people in when they first see it. Of course, the game must also be really solid, otherwise, their expectations will not be met.

Think about some games you've seen or played that draw your attention. It could be *Santorini*, *The Climbers*, *Rising Sun*, or one of many other games. Don't you want to know more and try them out just by looking at them?

It just so happens that these are great games as well. But it's that first initial reaction when you see a game on the table that makes you want to sit down and try it out.

First impressions are important.

So how do you make sure your game has a great table presence?

Well, you can start by thinking of some interesting components or board configurations that will get people's attention. The components could be miniatures, dragons, or meeples armed with equipment, like in the *Tiny Epic* series of games. Think of something that will stand out, be different than people have seen in other games, and will get others asking questions and wanting to know more. People can be captivated by toy-like components that really capture your imagination.

One other thing I've noticed is that height can be your friend. What do I mean by that? Games that have either a board or components that are elevated well above the tabletop can be very visually appealing.

*Santorini* has an elevated board, along with building pieces that increase the structure's height as you play. *The Climbers* uses building blocks that can reach a good height. *Fireball Island* has a raised board with a volcano in the center that sends fireballs all over the terrain.

Just by being raised well above the height of the table, these games attract attention from anyone walking by. This is especially the case where the height of the game is above the heads of the players at the table.

Of course, these examples may not apply so well to the game you're working on. If your game doesn't lend itself to a board or stacking components, then this may be a bit more of a challenge.

If you're working on a deckbuilder, another type of card game, or a game with minimal components, see if you can make those components more interesting and unique. Just think differently when you're crafting your deckbuilder, or at least make sure the art and graphic design are visually stunning (ultimately this is up to the publisher, but you can still use some great placeholders). Try to find ways to make your game stand out compared to others.

I am not that artistic, and this is an area where I struggle. Fortunately, I do have friends who are game designers and with whom I often co-design that are much better at this than me. Sometimes it's best to enlist help when needed.

For example, I had an idea for a game that is currently in development, called *Jewel Heist*. I knew that if this was done right, it would look fantastic on the table. I love working with my friend Sylvain (who always has great game ideas and suggestions) and knew that he was the one to help me make this happen, so I asked if he would co-design this game with me. It's not signed yet, but it has a couple of interested publishers and it looks fantastic!

I took this to Proto TO, a local game designer event, and everybody that walked by the game commented on how great it looked. It reminded them of *The Thomas Crown Affair*. That's exactly the reaction I was hoping for!

I'm definitely going to keep table presence at the top of my mind in all my future designs.

## Is That a Game or a Toy?

Not long ago we picked up *Forbidden Sky*. We own and quite enjoy the first two in the series (*Forbidden Island* and *Forbidden Desert*) and are big fans of designer Matt Leacock, so it was natural that we pick up this game as well.

After opening the box, we noticed there were quite a few interesting parts. I read the rules and discovered that you are actually connecting pieces to form a circuit to launch the rocket, which is the goal of the game.

We tried it out and found it quite challenging, which was exactly what we wanted. We didn't succeed in our first mission, but we just *had* to find out what happened when you did make a circuit and place the rocket on the launchpad. After fiddling around a bit to get the connection right, we got the pleasure of hearing the rocket make some cool takeoff noises.

It was pretty awesome to hear and I'm sure it would've been a satisfying ending had we completed the mission.

This got me thinking about what made that experience so intriguing. I had heard or read a few comments about *Forbidden Sky*, talking about it being both a toy and a game. Now I understood what they were saying.

There's a bit of childlike wonder in all of us, and we can still become fascinated by a simple toy.

I started delving back into much earlier games that could also be considered very toy-like.

Do you remember *Operation*, the game where you try to extract plastic pieces from a patient without setting off the buzzer?

How about *Hungry Hungry Hippos*, the smacking, slamming, marble chomping game?

Or *Mousetrap*? This one always looked really fun but I don't remember anybody actually wanting to play the game. We'd rather just try to set up the elaborate trap and see if it would actually work (spoiler: it usually didn't!).

There were several other games along these lines that didn't quite reach the same level of popularity. I remember one called *Don't Wake Daddy* and another one called *Let's Go Fishin'*, where you had to catch fish with little fishing poles as the pond rotated.

And who could forget *Perfection*? In this game, you had to place all these different shapes into the right spaces on the board before the timer went off and launched all the pieces flying.

But surely this fascination has passed, and nobody is creating games like this anymore, right? *Forbidden Sky* must be that rare exception. Or is it?

While maybe not as obvious or childish as *Operation* or *Mousetrap*, you can still see toy-like elements in some games being designed today. Don't believe me? Consider these examples…

*The Climbers*. Introduced in 2018, this game is all about climbing up the tower of blocks to try to be the first player to make it to the top. You do so by maneuvering around building blocks (who didn't play with these as a kid?)

and climbing little ladders. This game would be just as at home in a kindergarten class as it would at your gaming table.

Ever play *Junk Art*? This is a fun dexterity game, where you're placing different shaped objects like flowerpots and mini barbells to build towers that are either taller or remain standing longer than your opponent's.

How about *Santorini*? Yes, this game is very chess-like in its movements and strategy, and gets even more intricate with the use of the God cards that give players additional powers. But the main mechanics are building and climbing up and down towers made of cool plastic pieces. My 6-year-old self may not have been able to figure out the gameplay, but I sure would have loved to build those towers!

Still not convinced? How about *Fireball Island*? This game from the '80s was recently brought back to life by Restoration Games and features the rotating head of Vul-Kar, set atop a mountain, which launches fireballs (marbles) at anyone daring to steal treasures from the island. Players can also flick ember marbles at opponents to knock them over and steal their treasures. Again, the line between games and toys gets blurry. But who cares? It's so much fun!

How can you find ways to incorporate more fun, toy-like experiences in your games?

## Take Action

Write down why your game is different. Now think about how you could feature more of this or emphasize this better.

If you can't figure out what makes it unique, think about what you could do to make it more unique.

# 3

# Thinking about Your Game as a Product

> I'm always looking for something that's unique and stands out creatively… but most important is the commercial potential of the game; it needs to have a market.
>
> **– Richard MacRae, Analog Game Studios**

If you've created a great game that people love, this is a fantastic first step. However, when a publisher looks at your game they have to consider not only if it is a great game, but also how they will be able to sell it as a product.

One of my games I've been working on, called *Code Smashers,* has this problem. People love to play it and I've had two publishers take the prototype and really love it themselves, but so far, they haven't been able to come up with a way to market the game. I'm currently working with one of these publishers to see if we can re-theme it and make some slight changes to the mechanics to make it more accessible.

If you keep productization in mind while you're making a game, it will make this an easier sell for the publisher.

## Making Your Game More Publishable

One of the first things you want to consider before pitching your game to publishers is your intended audience. You need to know if your game is intended for the mass market, casual gamers, or hardcore gamers.

Will it appeal to kids? Families? Groups of friends? Adults only?

DOI: 10.1201/9781003334828-5

You want your game length to be just right for your game, a length that has players wanting more or at least doesn't overstay its welcome. You also need to make sure you have a compelling theme that matches well to the mechanics (although abstract can be ok too!).

Your game should have meaningful decisions. Players need to be given choices, but not just any choices. They shouldn't be obvious. There should be multiple paths a player can take but still stand a chance of winning.

You never want to have players feel like they made one bad choice early on and now they have no chance of winning, but still need to slog through another hour or two of your game just going through the motions. Those players will never play your game again.

Perception is really important. Even if your game is balanced just right, if multiple players complain about overpowering cards or imbalances in your game, you need to take note and dive into this further. Find out what feels out of place to the players and see if any adjustments are necessary.

You want your game to have plenty of strategies to get players thinking about what they'd do the next time they play. This doesn't mean that your game has to be complex or include a 32-page rulebook. In fact, many of the most popular games have a simple and elegant ruleset, but the way you play and choices you can make to create the strategic elements of your game (unless it's a party game – then you're aiming for fun and laughter).

What are people saying about your game? Are they asking to play again? Where they can buy it? These are good indications that you're on the right track and are getting closer to being able to pitch your game more successfully.

## Do You Really Need to Know How Much Your Game Will Cost?

"How much do you think this game will retail for?"

This was not a question that I was expecting to receive when I was showing *Isle of Rock n Roll* at a publisher speed dating event, but I was asked, nonetheless.

I had an idea in my mind of what the manufacturer's suggested retail price (MSRP) might be, but clearly, my estimate of $40–50 was too low.

The publisher immediately said there was no way the game could be made cheaply enough to justify that price. He went on to talk about the recent tariff hikes and the cost to produce wooden cubes, etc., and felt that my game had too many components.

Fair enough. There were tons of cubes, along with cards and a large board, among other things. I knew it wouldn't be a cheap game to produce, but it had such great table presence and it also played really well, so I felt that finding the right publisher would just be a matter of time.

Fortunately, I was correct.

Whereas some publishers saw a game that would be costly to produce, three other publishers took a keen interest in it and saw its potential. They talked about the ways they could reduce the board size and be able to sell it at a reasonable price, while still maintaining its uniqueness and table presence.

They looked past the overly polished prototype and loved the look, feel, and combination of mechanics that were both new and familiar.

While some saw issues, others recognized an opportunity.

## Do You Need to Know Your Game's MSRP?

So, the question comes back to whether or not you as a designer need to know what your game will sell for. Of course, if you are self-publishing, you must know this because you will be intimately involved in figuring out manufacturing, shipping, and everything else related to price.

But what if you're pitching your game to publishers?

This question has actually come up before in game design groups. One designer had received feedback from a judge in a game design competition they entered, and it was suggested that the designer should have put the MSRP on their sell sheet.

When he asked others if this was standard practice, the response was unanimous. Even those designers who have had a dozen games published have never once put an estimated MSRP on their sell sheet, nor have they been asked to do so.

It was clearly poor advice to request that any costs be included on a sell sheet. This is something the publisher will need to figure out.

And besides, if a publisher is large enough, they will have a developer who will ask the tough questions about whether each component is really necessary and will find ways to produce a really good-looking game within their budget. Or, they may contract out the development work. Either way, a good publisher will develop your game further and streamline anywhere they can.

But that doesn't mean you shouldn't be thinking about component costs.

## What You Do Need to Keep in Mind

Even though it will be the publisher who is responsible for figuring out the manufacturing and retail costs, as a designer, it is still important for you to think about them as well.

Here are some things to consider:

1. You want to make sure that the price of your game will be in the range of the publisher or publishers you're interested in pitching your game to. If they only do small box games under $20, then it is highly unlikely they will take an interest in your miniatures game that will retail for over $100.
2. Look at ways you can reduce component counts. If you can use both sides of a card or board or put multiple topics on one card in the case of a party game, for example, these are good ways to reduce costs and make your game more appealing to a publisher.
3. List your components on your sell sheet. Now look at this list and determine if every one of them is necessary. Also, you don't have to get into the details of how many event cards, power cards, reference cards, etc. you have, but rather just list how many standard-size cards, mini cards, boards (along with a rough size), cubes, meeples, and other components you've included. This will help a publisher, who is much more familiar with the cost than you, determine the rough production and retail cost.

## How to Estimate Costs

A quick rule of thumb is that a game will sell for approximately five times the manufacturing cost.

So, if your game costs $10 to produce, it will likely sell for around $50. But how do you know what the manufacturing cost will be?

Well, you can ask for an estimate from a board game manufacturer. They can give you quotes on multiple quantities, typically with a minimum of 500 or 1,000 copies. You will see that the prices go down per game as the quantity goes up.

You could even just ask for quotes for each different component that you use. For example, ask about the cost per card, meeple, cube, token, etc. Make sure to also include the box, which is often the most expensive part to manufacture. And make sure that the manufacturer quotes for a box that is big enough to hold everything, including cards that have been sleeved, and any insert or cavity you'd want to include.

However, if you have zero intention of self-publishing the game, recognize you are taking up time that they could be spending quoting a project from someone who is ready to publish their game. If you can get just one quote for a hypothetical game with all possible components you may need with a complete breakdown of this or ask someone who has gone through this process already, it can be used to help you estimate component costs for this and all your future games.

Another method some designers use is to price all the components on The Game Crafter (thegamecrafter.com). The cost to get your game made here will be somewhere in the same ballpark as what your game would need to retail for (not the manufacturing cost).

To sum this all up, you don't need to know exactly how much your game will sell for, but it definitely is helpful to have a rough idea of how much it would cost to produce your game, and therefore what it might sell for. This helps you to get into the mind of a publisher and think about where you can save some costs or reduce unnecessary components, without negatively affecting the overall player experience.

## Being a Publisher Means Running a Business (Your Game Is a Product)

Publishers want not only a game that's really good but also one that will SELL. You have to keep in mind that publishers are running a business, and the only way they can stay in business is if they can sell what they create to make money.

This is such an important thing to remember. It can change the way you design (for the better).

A publisher might love your game but not know how they can market it. This has happened to me multiple times. Either a publisher rejects a game (even if they love the game itself) or they want me to re-theme it to something that will sell more easily. Sometimes a publisher will take on the re-theming themselves, and other times they will ask the designer to come up with a new take on their own game.

If the publisher doesn't feel they will be able to market your game as it currently stands, it may be a pass for them.

If this happens to you, go back to thinking about what makes your game unique and if there is some other way to make it stand out. This may be a re-theme or an overhaul of one aspect that the publisher has defined as "difficult to market."

What is your game's unique selling proposition? What makes it stand out? What got that publisher's attention in the first place? Now, put yourself in the publisher's shoes and think about how you would be able to market and sell your game if you had to.

## Branding Is Important

Another important consideration is branding. If you look at a publisher's current catalog, there is likely one game (or maybe a few games if they are a larger publisher) that is outselling all their other games by a decent margin.

Publishers are often risk-averse. They would rather go with something they know will do well than take a big chance on something new and unproven.

Another version or spin-off of *Pandemic* might not sell as many copies as the original, but it will likely sell more than some random new game idea. That's why many publishers opt for expansions and different versions of their own hit games.

So, I want you to think about how your game could fit into an existing brand. Maybe a few minor changes would help your game to fit into another game's universe. If your game could be an offshoot of another hit game, why wouldn't the publisher be interested in hearing more about your game?

If you go this route, I would advise you to contact the designer of the original game first before approaching the publisher, if possible. You may have the opportunity to co-design with an established designer who already has the publisher's ear, or at least get their blessing for you to approach the publisher.

Keep in mind that if you've done all the work, you won't want to hand off 50% of the royalties to someone else who is just putting their name on it, but if you bring them on board early enough and you both contribute substantially to the game, this could be very beneficial to both of you. However, just letting the designer know and getting their blessing can be a great approach, as you won't have to worry about stepping on anyone's toes!

## Take Action

Write down why you think a publisher would be interested in your game. Now, start to get a feel for what your game will cost to produce and what it would sell for based on the five times MSRP formula. Where does this put your game in terms of price range? Is this reasonable for the complexity, audience, and game length?

Now consider any possible brands your game could fall under. Are there any changes you could make to help your game match a successful existing brand?

# 4

# The Importance of Playtesting

> Designers often try to pitch a game that is not yet ready. A game should have received extensive playtesting and revisions with multiple groups that have no connection to the designer, and of the correct target audience.
>
> **– Curt Covert, Smirk & Dagger Games**

"I have this great business idea," he said.

This was the start of a conversation with a friend of mine. It was something he came up with and wanted to make a reality. He really wanted to leave his day job and start his own business. After brainstorming over 100 different business ideas, this was the one he felt most passionate about.

He then went on in great detail about how it would work and how excited he was about the idea. He imagined it revolutionizing the way that medications and other health products were delivered to customers.

That was 3 years ago.

So, how is his business doing now you ask?

Well, would you believe that it's still just an idea sitting in his head waiting to be developed? It never even got off the ground.

Unfortunately, this is all too common. People talk about ideas, but very few put them into action.

## Your Game Idea Is Worthless … Until You Do This

But what does this have to do with game design? Well, quite a bit actually.

DOI: 10.1201/9781003334828-6

You see, every game starts as an idea. But like anything else, whether it's a business idea, creative endeavor, or a New Year's resolution, quite often that's also where it ends.

Coming up with ideas is the easy part. Taking action and turning them into something tangible is the hard part.

That's why many of us keep a long list of ideas of things we want to do, but we rarely make a significant dent in this list.

It's so important to take the time and effort to turn that idea into something real. When it comes to a game, that means putting together the simplest prototype possible and testing it out.

Even if it looks like this.

**An early prototype of one of my games, *Playing Chicken*, using a standard deck of cards, a handful of quickly created goal cards, and coins stolen from Machi Koro**

The longer your idea just sits in your head, the less chance you will actually do something with it. It's even worse if you don't write it down. If your memory is anything like mine, it will probably be forgotten by the next day (unless it's an idea I just can't stop thinking about!).

Put something simple together and try it out. See what works. See what doesn't. There may be a lot of things not working initially, but that's ok. This is where you work out the kinks and start to make early improvements.

Then, get it in front of other people.

Start with family, friends, and anyone else willing to give it a try. As it develops, you'll continue playtesting it with other designers, strangers, and anyone else who doesn't run away when you pull out the box.

One of the biggest concerns that new designers have (including me when I was starting out) is having their idea stolen. I mention this often when people ask about getting into the hobby, and it's something important I feel I need to continue to talk about to help new designers move forward and not get stuck in such an early stage.

Getting your game playtested by others is so crucial for getting valuable feedback to improve your game. This means getting it in front of as many people as possible, particularly other game designers and your core audience.

If you're afraid to play your game with others, your game will not improve. At least not to the point where it's going to be able to compete against all the other great games on the market.

Other game designers have their own games they're working on. They have enough to keep them busy without needing to steal ideas from others. Besides, most people love their own ideas best and would prefer to focus on something they came up with themselves.

Most other people will never make their own game. They may enjoy playing games a lot, but extremely few of them will ever get into game design. Some may like the idea of creating their own game but aren't willing to put in the time and effort to make something themselves. And that's totally fine. Not everybody can be a game designer. But that's also good for you because you don't have to worry about them stealing your ideas.

Finally, there's your reputation at stake. The game design community is a small and tight-knit one. You'd have a hard time finding playtesters and publishers interested in your game if you were known as a thief.

Getting started is always the hardest part of doing anything. Once you get started, it always gets easier and you'll wonder why you didn't start sooner.

## Get a Feel for What Is Working and What Is Not

Throughout your playtesting, you want to observe what players are doing, both when it is their turn, and when they're waiting for their turn. Notice whether players are engaged or if they are distracted and doing other things like checking their phones.

Take plenty of notes on what you see and how you feel as you either play or observe the game.

Make sure to thank your playtesters profusely for their time and make it a comfortable atmosphere for them to provide you with honest feedback.

## Ask the Right Questions

After you playtest your game, you're going to ask some questions of your playtesters.

Some designers just go around the table asking each person their opinion. While this can sometimes be helpful, I find it's usually more useful if you have specific questions you can ask of the group.

What questions you ask will depend on the stage of your game. If it's still early on, you may just be trying to figure out what's working and what's not. But as your game moves further along, you'll want to ask more targeted questions.

Here are a few that I use regularly:

- What was the most fun part of the game?
- What part of the game did you like the least?
- If you could change one aspect of the game to make it better, what would it be?
- Do you feel like you deserved to win (to the winner)?
- Do you feel like you had a chance to win (to all the others)?
- Is this a game you would want to play again?

These questions are generally good at most stages, and you can add any additional questions about any specific mechanics or recent changes you've made to the game to see if they have improved.

## Take Feedback Gracefully

When you put your game in front of strangers, they may be more forthcoming with criticism than people you already know.

Just keep this in mind: Your playtesters are not criticizing *you* or your ability to make games. So, you have to learn not to take it personally or get defensive.

Write down all the feedback you receive and ask probing questions to dive deeper into anything that is unclear or requires further information.

You don't have to incorporate every suggestion playtesters make (as they may often contradict other suggestions) but be sure to thank everyone for their feedback and let them know that you appreciate their suggestions and for taking the time to play your game.

This will definitely increase the chances that they will play this game or a future game of yours again.

## Decipher Feedback, and Look for Trends and Patterns

When you're receiving feedback from playtesters, you want to look for common trends.

If you receive a one-off comment about something specific that nobody else mentions, this may not be as relevant.

However, if multiple people are telling you that the turns take too long or you are continuously seeing people turning to their cell phones when it's not their turn, you know you have a problem to address.

Also, watch out for playtesters (especially other game designers) who make suggestions to turn your game into the game that they want to play or create themselves. While an idea may be interesting, if it takes your game away from your original vision, you'll want to treat this carefully.

## Make Changes to Your Game

Now, take that feedback you've received and try to understand what the biggest problem is in your game.

Brainstorm several possible solutions rather than just going with the first one that comes to mind, then determine which one has the most potential. Try making this change and see if your game improves. If not, go back to your list and find the next best option. Continue in this manner until the problem has been solved.

You can then repeat this process with any other issues identified in your game. I'd suggest doing this one at a time if possible so that you can more easily identify what has improved your game. Sometimes you'll find that making one change can improve multiple aspects at the same time.

## Repeat

Now, you're going to repeat this process with other playtest groups, gathering feedback, and making changes to your game.

You'll notice over time that your game is improving and becoming a better experience for your players. Don't get discouraged if that change you implemented doesn't make your game better immediately. Just revert to the previous version or try another solution to any of the problems you've identified.

You'll continue this process until your game is running smoothly on a consistent basis. Once you're no longer receiving suggestions on how to make your game better, but rather the ideas you are hearing will just make your game different, you'll know you're getting closer to the end.

When players start asking when they can buy your game, then you really know you're on the right track.

## Take Action

Continue to playtest your game and make changes to improve it (hopefully) for the better. Once your game is playing well consistently and people are asking to buy it, it's time to move forward with documenting your rules and getting everything ready for you to pitch to publishers.

# 5

# How to Write Your Rule Book Without Getting a Headache

Continue to make games. This may not connect to success, but it becomes the power behind designing great games.

**– Seiji Kanai**

One of the biggest challenges game designers face is **creating a good rule book**.

It's funny. You'd think that the person who created the game would be in the best position to write the rules and that it should come easy, especially after teaching the game so many times.

But the reality is, it's really hard.

And what do you think happens to a game with a terrible rulebook (or even rules that have a few flaws)?

I think we both know the answer to that question!

Nobody plays that game. It sits on the shelf and never gets any love.

Do you want your game to suffer the same fate?

I *know* we both know the answer to that question.

So, let's go back to that teaching aspect for a second. You've had to explain your game many times to different players, so there must be some way you can use this to your advantage.

In just a moment, I'll show you a great technique the pros use that you can easily utilize to write your rulebook quickly.

DOI: 10.1201/9781003334828-7

## Write Out the Steps in Your Game

Once you've run many playtests and your game is running smoothly, the next step is to ensure that your game will be just as engaging and as well understood when you're not there.

First, you can start by documenting the steps needed to get your game set up, followed by what players do in your game.

I suggest using the following order:

1. Components
2. What your game is about and the roles of all players (intro and theme)
3. How to win (goal/objective)
4. Set up (including pictures of the layout to get players started)
5. How to play (including examples and visuals)
6. Things to keep in mind during the game
7. Exceptions ("weird" scenarios and clarifications)
8. Scoring and endgame (determining the winner, tie-breaker, etc)
9. Notes for easy reference (a reminder section for players to refer to for key points)
10. A legend, including icons, terminology, and anything else of importance

## Document Your Rules the Same Way You Teach Them

There's probably a natural order in which you explain your game to others. You likely (and really should) start with what the game is about, what roles players take on, and the objective (i.e. how you win the game).

You probably follow this up with what players can do on their turn and how rounds or phases play out. If you're a really good teacher, you give examples as well.

So, why not start by documenting your rules in the same order and flow that you would teach them? If this makes the most sense to the players in front of you, it will also help to teach players your game when you're not there.

## How to Record Your Rules Like a Pro

Here's a pro tip that I picked up, and frankly one that I should make more use of myself.

Here it is: record yourself explaining the rules. It's so simple. Yet so effective.

As game designers, we sometimes overcomplicate things. Why not make this difficult task a bit easier on yourself?

Simply record yourself or have someone else record you explaining your game to others. Then use this recording to transcribe the first draft of your rules.

Want to do this even faster?

Talk into a speech recognition program such as Dragon Naturally Speaking, and have your rules documented automatically. There are other free programs online including Speech Notes (speechnotes.co/), Speech Texter (speechtexter.com/), Google Keyboard (tinyurl.com/gookey), and a function in Google Docs that you can use as well.

Of course, you'll still need to edit your rules and move things around a bit, but when you record yourself, you'll have a huge head start. No more staring at your screen wondering how to explain your rules.

## A Picture Is Worth a Thousand Words

Think about how different players learn. Many people are visual learners, so it is always helpful to include lots of diagrams in your rules.

Make sure to include the starting setup so that players can easily see how the game should look on the table right from the start. This gives players the confidence that they've done everything right and are ready to go.

Also, ensure that players can understand actions they can take, along with any restrictions, through the use of visual aids. Anything that players can do should be shown clearly through imagery.

## Make an Example of Your Rules

Examples can also be incredibly helpful. Along with visuals for the layout and player actions, it's extremely beneficial to include examples to show players what they can and cannot do. For example, if they decide to explore, show them how they may place the tile in certain specific locations (but also note where it cannot be placed).

In video games, the game itself enforces these rules, but in board games, this is much more difficult to govern.

These examples should show players exactly what happens in different situations. They can even walk players through what happens throughout someone's turn.

When players can understand what happens and when, especially under different circumstances, this will ensure that the rules are followed properly and that nothing is missed. If a player can choose from multiple options in different situations, show the players what this looks like.

For example, you could say, "Lisa uses her first action to explore and places a new tile adjacent to her. She uses her second action to move to that tile and her third and final action to search. When she searches, she picks up a tool card, and places this card face-up in front of her for later use."

It's also recommended that you include player aids. These could be sheets or reference cards that help players to understand what they can do on their turn.

Explain all the steps through your words and images, and you'll have players thanking you for having such an easy to follow rulebook.

## The Blind Leading the Blind

Don't trust that the rules you've written will be easily understood. You must put your rules in front of players who have never played your game before and see how well they do without any help on your part.

This is known as blind playtesting, and it's a critical step in game design.

The players should be given the box and have to set up the game and learn the rules in a way that is fully understood by all players.

When you sit back and observe, you'll be surprised at how many rules are missed or misunderstood!

It's your job to stay quiet, take notes, and then go back and revise your rules to clarify anything that was done incorrectly, as well as make changes if players did something that you realized was actually better or more intuitive. Continue this process until your game plays smoothly and no rules are being misinterpreted.

We'll go into this more in-depth in the next chapter.

## Read Everything Over and Follow the Steps to Make Sure It Makes Sense

Once your rules are written, try to set up and play your game following these rules. Note any places where you missed any steps and go back and update these sections.

See if there are any places where more examples or visuals would help a new player get started and make sure to include these in your rules. You don't want your rulebook to be too long, but at the same time, a short rulebook that doesn't explain your game well enough for players to learn your game properly is no benefit either.

## Have Others Read Over Your Rules (Those Who Have and Haven't Played Your Game)

Once you feel like your rules are in pretty good shape, ask others to read them over to see if they make sense.

You can do this with others who have played your game so that they can help identify anything that may have been missed, as well as with new players, to see if they understand how the game is played.

You can also ask someone new to your game to read over the rules and explain them back to you to make sure your rules make sense when you hear them explained out loud.

Anything unclear or previously left out should now be updated in your rules.

## Take Action

Determine the method you are going to use to document your rules (speech to text, recording audio, writing). Now, set up your board game and go through all the steps you would normally go through when teaching your game. Make use of the ordered steps provided in this chapter if needed. Record your rules. Now, review them and make sure you didn't miss anything of importance. You'll be using these rules for the blind playtests you'll set up in the next chapter.

# 6

# How and Why You Need to Blind Playtest Your Game

> The real test, to see if your game is any good, is to get it out there and let it be played by people who don't know you personally. Don't be afraid of their critiques.
>
> **– Adrian Ademescu**

So, your game runs smoothly when you teach it to other players, but what happens when you're not there?

One thing that all designers have to keep in mind is that when somebody buys a game and takes it home, they'll have to learn it on their own or from someone else, and you won't be there to help them or correct any mistakes.

That's why it's crucial to not only create well-written rules but also blind playtest these rules with multiple groups.

Here's how the process works.

## Hand Over the Game Box With Your Rules

First, you'll want to find a group of players who have never played your game. Even if one person has played it in the past and remembers your game at all, this playtest will not give you all the information you need to bring your game closer to completion.

Next, you're going to hand over the box with your game, rules, and all components to the group. You won't explain how to set up or play your game, as this will be up to the players to decipher.

DOI: 10.1201/9781003334828-8

Have one player read through the rules so that the group can set up your game and let them explain your game to the rest of the group.

Let the games begin!

## Avoid the Temptation to Interfere

Unlike previous playtests where you answered players' questions and helped them to understand what they could and couldn't do in your game, with blind playtesting, you're going to act as if you aren't even there.

It is completely up to the players to set up and play your game without your help. If they have any questions, just shrug and ask them what the rulebook says.

It would be even more ideal to run your blind playtest when you're not even there. By recording the playtest or having someone else run it (and optionally record this as well), you can gather even more information. That way, you can watch sections of playtests over and over to understand what players are feeling and how they interact with your game. However, this is not always possible, so the next best thing you can do is sit back, observe, and take lots of notes.

## Note Anything Not Set Up or Followed Correctly

While the players are setting up your game, watch exactly how they do it and make note of anything that is done incorrectly, out of order, or put in the wrong place.

Once the game begins, you'll continue to observe and take notes about anything the players find confusing, is being done wrong, or requires repeated referencing of the rules.

It's going to be really hard, but you need to hold yourself back from interjecting or correcting anything the players are doing. Pretend this is a science experiment and you are on the other side of a glass panel without access to your guinea pigs—uh, I mean players.

Blind playtesting your game is going to give you so many insights. You'll see where your rules are unclear

You will identify any steps you missed or are out of order

You may find that you have some clunky rules or exceptions that don't need to be part of your game

You may see ways to improve or change rules that are more intuitive to players

You'll also see how players think and where more examples or images could be beneficial.

## Take Action

Ok, it's time to blind playtest your game. Hand over the box with all components and rules to a group of new players and watch as they try to figure it out. If you can, record this, and/or have someone else run the blind playtest (although this is not crucial). Take lots of notes so that you can improve your rules further and make it much easier for future players. Then, update your rules accordingly and repeat this process to ensure that players fully understand how to play your game.

# 7

# Should You Pitch to Publishers or Self-Publish?

Stay patient but stay hungry.

**– Chris Chung**

As I mentioned earlier, this book is focused on how to pitch your game to publishers successfully, NOT how to crowdfund or otherwise self-publish your game.

I talk about the differences between publishing a game yourself and letting a publisher do the work in great detail in The Board Game Designer's Guide (tinyurl.com/bgdguide), and there are some great resources you can use if you're thinking about self-publishing, such as Jamey Stegmaier's excellent Kickstarter Lessons blog (tinyurl.com/kslessons) and book, A Crowdfunder's Strategy Guide (tinyurl.com/crowdguide).

So, I'll just quickly summarize the pros and cons of pitching your game to publishers, along with the risks and rewards of self-publishing from my previous book here, so that we see the differences. Then we can get right into putting together what you need to successfully pitch your game to publishers.

## First, the Pros

There are a lot of benefits to having a publisher produce your game, that is if you are lucky enough to have one interested in signing it. Many publishers get hundreds (if not thousands) of submissions each year and may only release a few of these.

DOI: 10.1201/9781003334828-9

But if a publisher does release your game, the great thing is, they will do all the heavy lifting, including getting the game manufactured, marketed, and into the big retail stores and/or game shops where people can easily find them. By not having to worry about these responsibilities, you can focus your time on designing more games.

You can also expect a larger print run and more reach, especially with larger publishers, as they will often do a print run of 5,000–10,000 games or more, with the possibility of additional print runs if there's enough demand. A typical game successfully funded on Kickstarter, on the other hand, may only generate a print run of 1,000–2,000 games. For a self-publisher, this is considered pretty successful. Your game will usually get much more exposure by working with a publisher, plus you will get royalties for every copy sold.

## Now, the Cons

There are some downsides to traditional publishing though. One of the big ones is the loss of creative control. Once you sign over your game to a publisher, they have the right to change the theme, mechanics, and even the name of your game. If maintaining creative control over your vision is the most important thing to you, this may not be ideal.

There's also a chance that your game will never see the light of day. The timing may be off, or they may just choose to go a different direction, leaving your game on the shelf for an extended period of time.

Also, don't expect to make a ton of money. Unless your game becomes the next *Ticket to Ride* or *Settlers of Catan*, you probably won't be retiring anytime soon.

## The Risks and Rewards of Self-Publishing

Make no mistake about it, if you self-publish a game, you are now running a business. You'll want to be really sure that this is right for you before making this jump. You'll actually end up spending way more time on the business aspects, and a lot less on actual game design.

You'll maintain creative control and be able to produce your game any way you choose.

There's a hidden risk in this, in that you may end up losing your passion for creating board games by being bogged down with all of the business responsibilities. However, if you love business, or the idea of running your own business, great! You may end up finding this very fulfilling.

## Take Action

If you're favoring pitching to publishers and eager to learn how to do so effectively, then let's jump right into this in the next section.

# Section II

# Everything You Need before You Pitch to Publishers

# 8

# First, What You Don't Need

> The better you know the publisher and how they work, the better you can focus on how to best present your game.
>
> **– Alexander Pfister**

Before we get into what you need to increase your chances of successfully pitching your game, let's quickly look at what you don't need so that you can save yourself a lot of time.

## Art

The game you're pitching is a prototype, not a final product. Keep in mind that any publisher who signs your game will have all the rights to it and be able to change it in any way they choose. Most publishers are more attracted to the mechanics, but the theme can also help to draw them in.

This includes any art or graphic design that you provide. So, don't hire an artist. Don't spend money on a graphic designer. All these costs will be lost, and the publisher will go with whomever they choose (either in-house or contracted out).

Use whatever free art and icons you can find, and let the publisher know that this is just placeholder art. This will convey the look and feel of your game to help give the publisher a direction to take with your game. Note that while a game doesn't need to look amazing at this stage, it certainly can help to get a publisher's attention.

DOI: 10.1201/9781003334828-11

## Trademarks

Trademarks are both costly and time-consuming to obtain. Not to mention the fact that every region has its own submission process and fee.

They are also completely unnecessary if you are pitching your game to a publisher. In fact, if a publisher wants to put a trademark on your game once they've got the rights to it, they can. They may place this under your name or their own. This is the publisher's choice.

So, obtaining your own trademark just complicates matters. It may also make you look like a bit of a rookie, so I'd strongly advise against trying to get a trademark for your game.

## Non-Disclosure Agreements

No. No. No.

Never ask a publisher to sign a non-disclosure agreement. They are not trying to steal your idea and it's incredibly rare for something like this to ever come up. It would hurt the publisher's reputation and you'd likely be able to prove you had created the game first if you've documented it, so just don't go this route.

A publisher is likely to walk away if you ask them to sign a non-disclosure agreement. It could turn out they are already working on a game that has similarities to yours. They need to protect themselves from this type of situation.

Now, on the other hand, a publisher may ask *you* to sign a non-disclosure agreement. Again, this is to protect them in the case that they already have something similar in the works. Generally, this should not be a concern for you to sign.

As a game designer, the only way to make your game better is by getting it out in front of players and getting feedback to make it the best game it can be. The same goes for pitching your game to publishers. You need to hear what an experienced publisher thinks of your game so that you can get it published one day, either with them or with another publisher.

So, in case I wasn't clear, never ask a publisher to sign a non-disclosure agreement!

## Take Action

Make sure your prototype conveys your game and theme well. Ensure your icons and symbols make sense and that players understand what they mean. Now, let's move on to what you need to prepare to pitch to publishers successfully.

# 9

# Become Pitch-Perfect (or at Least Pitch-Great)

If you aren't excited about it, why should I be?

**– Cody Thompson, Gold Nugget Games**

So, your game is awesome, and people are asking when they can buy it. Your rules are crisp and clear after several rounds of blind playtesting.

Now, how do you get a publisher's attention when they're already drowning in game submissions?

Many of us game designers (including me) are introverts. So, pitching your game to publishers probably doesn't come naturally to you.

Do you struggle to come up with a hook and an elevator pitch for your game?

Does the thought of trying to "sell" your game to a complete stranger raise your anxiety through the roof?

It doesn't have to leave you a bundle of nerves. With a bit of practice, you can feel calm and confident the next time you meet with a publisher to show them your game.

So many designers end up in front of a publisher and don't know what to say or how to present their game in a way that will get the publisher excited.

Your pitch shouldn't be an afterthought, rather it must be a concise, compelling narrative about your game that will have publishers asking for more.

Let's look at how to structure this in a few easy sentences that will captivate your audience.

DOI: 10.1201/9781003334828-12

## The Elevator Pitch: You Have 30 Seconds to Get a Publisher Interested

Your elevator pitch is something you need to develop if you want to get the attention of that publisher you've been courting. You may only have minutes or even seconds to talk to someone at their booth or an event, so how do you get them asking for more?

Let's take an in-depth look at what you need to have ready once you have the publisher's undivided attention with your captivating elevator pitch.

We, game designers, sometimes talk in terms that no one outside our industry would ever understand. We can even confuse most casual gamers in the way we describe things.

Tell me which one sounds more appealing to you:

"It's a worker placement game with aspects of economics and hand management."

OR

"Players find themselves in the roles of people in rustic, pre-modern Tuscany who have inherited meager vineyards. They have a few plots of land, an old crush pad, a tiny cellar, and three workers. They each have a dream of being the first to call their winery a true success."

The first one sounds like a board game sommelier. And not a very compelling one.

The second description talks a lot more about what the game is actually about and intrigues you to want to play.

Both are accurate descriptions of the game *Viticulture* by Jamey Stegmaier. Yet one is clearly more appealing. I actually pulled the latter from the Boardgamegeek description (tinyurl.com/bggviticulture) (good job, Jamey!).

Viticulture, by Jamey Stegmaier

## Elements of a Good Pitch

Whether you're pitching your game to a publisher or trying to find interested playtesters, you need to be able to distill your game down into a short elevator pitch. And it has to be one that will get people interested in your game.

Rather than talk about the mechanics of your game, focus on the following:

- What roles can players take on?
- What is the setting of your game?
- What do players do in your game or what's available to them?
- What is the objective of your game?
- What makes your game unique?

Let's see how the second description of *Viticulture* accomplishes this:

- Players find themselves in the roles of people in rustic, pre-modern Tuscany who have inherited meager vineyards (**covering both the roles and setting**)
- They have a few plots of land, an old crush pad, a tiny cellar, and three workers (**what's available to them**)
- They each have a dream of being the first to call their winery a true success (**the objective and what makes this unique)**

Do you see how describing your game in this way would appeal to more people?

Rather than sounding mechanical and clunky, you're drawing people in by showing them the experience they will have. Will this make everyone want to play your game? Not necessarily. Everyone likes different kinds of games, so no matter how well you describe yours, it may not be someone's cup of tea. But at least you'll bring in a lot more of the gamers who are more likely to want to try, and perhaps even buy, your game.

## One More Example

Think about how you would pitch other games in your collection. For example, if I wanted to convince someone to try *Pandemic*, I'd say something like:

"As members of the CDC (Centers for Disease Control and Prevention), we've been tasked with stopping a global outbreak of four deadly diseases.

As a team, we'll need to travel around the world, gathering intelligence and stopping the spread of the diseases, by curing each one of them before time runs out. Each one of us will play a different role and have unique abilities we need to use to save the world."

## The 2-Minute Pitch

Once you have the publisher's attention with your elevator pitch and they are asking for you to tell them more, it's time to move on to your 2-minute pitch.

During your 2-minute pitch, you'll have a bit more time to explain exactly what happens on a player's turn. Go through what a player can do on their turn and what types of choices they get to make.

In the example of *Pandemic*, you could say:

"On your turn, you'll need to coordinate with your fellow team members to figure out what the priorities are and how you can best use everyone's abilities to tackle the growing threats. You can travel between connected cities, treat diseases, open up new research facilities, and gather intel so you can find a cure for these diseases before they take over the earth."

"Every player has a special ability that will allow them to do things like treat diseases faster, dispatch other players around the board, and find cures more quickly. But after every player's turn, you run the risk of an epidemic, which will cause more cities to get infected. This can lead to outbreaks, which spread the diseases further. If the outbreaks aren't controlled, or you take too much time, your team will lose."

"There's a constant tension, as you have to make difficult decisions between tackling the spreading diseases (which will cause you to lose if they get out of control) and finding all the cures (which is required to win). You ignore one at the peril of the other."

If you've never played *Pandemic* before, wouldn't you want to now?

## How to Demo Your Game Effectively

If you've practiced your pitches well and the publisher is a good fit for your game, they may request to set up a time to demo your game.

If possible, make sure you arrive early to set up your game and that you have everything ready to go. If the demo will be at their booth or somewhere else you can't access early to set up, just have all your components ready, decks shuffled and set up, and everything else as close to ready as possible.

Many designers, myself included, recommend "stacking the deck", so to speak, meaning that the scenario, cards, and anything else are arranged to deliver a great experience. You want to give the best first impression.

If you have cards that might cause any confusion or edge cases, try to avoid them. Instead, put some of the most interesting cards at the top of the deck. This will give the publisher a feel for some of the most engaging moments that can occur in the game.

Know exactly how much time you have with the publisher and demo your game accordingly. It's great if your game is short and you have the opportunity to play from start to finish, but quite often this will not be the case.

If there's not enough time to do a full playthrough, just walk through what happens in a round, or at least on a player's turn. Go through all the interesting and exciting things that players can do in your game.

If you're able to demonstrate some of the really fun or engaging moments in your game, you'll have a stronger chance of getting the publisher's interest and maybe they'll even ask if they can take your prototype home with them.

I've pitched my games to dozens of publishers in the past few years, through email, one-on-one meetings, and publisher speed dating events. Some have been scheduled meetings, whereas other times I've approached a publisher at a booth or event, introduced myself, and given a quick elevator pitch for my games. I've been amazed at the success that can come with being prepared and putting yourself out there.

## Take Action

Create your elevator pitch for your game. Just follow the prompts above to outline the roles players take on, the setting, what players do, the objective, and what makes your game unique. Keep it short and punchy!

Now expand on that to create your 2-minute pitch. Go into more detail and talk more about some of the interesting choices and scenarios that can come up in your game.

# 10

# How to Create a Sell Sheet That Will Actually Sell Your Game

> It should have a broad-stroke overview of the game theme and core mechanics. The number of players, age, play length. But most importantly, in that description, what is the hook that leaves me excited and interested to learn more.
>
> **– Curt Covert, Smirk & Dagger Games**

You've created a great game. You've playtested it like crazy. You've even run some successful blind playtests.

You've decided that Kickstarter isn't your thing and you don't want to self-publish. So now it's up to you to find a publisher for your game.

You're going to need to make a sell sheet. This is a one-page summary of your game that will act like a pitch that you can give to a publisher at a meeting, convention, speed dating event, or via email.

Think of your sell sheet as a resume. If you do a good job with this and have a potential publisher in mind, it will help you to get your foot in the door and have them look at your game (kind of like entering the interview stage for a job).

But what makes a good sell sheet?

And what if you have no graphic design skills whatsoever (just like me)?

Why in the world would a publisher give your sell sheet a second look when everyone else's sell sheets look so much better?

Publishers *will* look at your sell sheet and be interested in your game, not because your sell sheet is flashy, but because they are a great match for your game and *you've included everything they need to know* in a well-laid-out manner (believe me, publishers really appreciate this!).

DOI: 10.1201/9781003334828-13

I'm going to break this down step-by-step, so you can finally feel confident in your sell sheet.

## What You Need to Include

There are a number of important details you'll want to include in your sell sheet. Here's a rundown of exactly what you'll need:

### *The Name of Your Game*

Ok, this is a pretty straightforward one. This should be right up at the top of your sell sheet and easy to read. Try not to use any fancy fonts that could be difficult to decipher. Of course, it never hurts to have a strong, interesting, and compelling name.

### *Your Contact Information*

Again, this should be pretty obvious, but you'd be surprised how many times a publisher has been really interested in a game and the designer didn't even leave so much as their own name!

At a bare minimum, include your name, email, and the best phone number to reach you. It's not a bad idea to include your address as well.

### *The Hook*

Make sure to express what makes your game unique and compelling. Why would the publisher be interested in signing your game? What makes your game stand out from all the others on the market?

This is preferably accomplished through a tagline or subtitle but may be placed somewhere else where it will stand out on your sell sheet.

### *Demographics*

You'll want to let the publisher know the three main pieces of demographic information:

1. Player count
2. Expected age range, and
3. Estimated play time of your game

Look at almost any board game box and you'll find all this information.

Including these details will help a publisher quickly determine if this game is the right fit for them. If your game is for adults 18 and up, a publisher focusing on making family-friendly games will know right away this isn't a good match (which saves both you and the publisher a lot of wasted time).

### *Components*

Make sure to include a list of all the components required to play your game. This doesn't have to break out every single detail. For example, you don't have to say 25 attack cards, 20 magic cards, 18 health cards, 12 special cards, and 25 equipment cards, unless each of the cards has different dimensions. Just say 100 standard size cards (or whatever size you're using).

Including this list of components will allow a publisher to get a rough idea of the manufacturing cost, which will let them estimate what they would price the game at, and if this would be in line with their expectations. The final components will likely change before the game is published, but at the very least this information gives the publisher something to work with.

### *What's Your Game About?*

Give a brief overview of what role players will take on in your game, along with what they're trying to accomplish. Make sure to include anything unique or clever about your game.

### *An Explanation of How the Game Is Played, Including Pictures or Images*

It will be important for the publisher to see how your game is played. Rather than get into the mechanics and the nitty-gritty details of all the rules, just give a quick overview of what happens in the game or on a player's turn. A publisher will understand what mechanics are involved or will ask about this if they're interested.

Your description should include a sample round, indicating what players do on their turn, and possible options they may have.

It's really helpful to include some images so that publishers get a feel for the style, gameplay, and components.

## Anything Else?

If there's anything else that makes a game special, make sure to include this in the sell sheet. Just don't overdo it.

Make sure everything is legible, the font is large enough to read, and you've included all the important information. Make it visually appealing and not too wordy. No one likes to read a wall of text!

If you've done a good job on your sell sheet and present it to a publisher that is potentially a good fit for your game, you may be contacted for more information, or they may even request a prototype of your game.

## What You'll Want to Leave Out

Now you know what you should include in your sell sheet, but it's also important to understand what you should leave out.

Remember, this is not a detailed rule summary. I made the mistake on some of my early sell sheets of going far too deep into the rules, way more than necessary.

Give the publisher just enough to whet their appetite but leave them wanting more.

Also, don't go deep into the back story, or how you came up with the game. No publisher cares if you've been working on this for the last 10 years. In fact, that may actually be a red flag for them, as they may wonder why it took so long to develop your game.

Stick to the facts.

Avoid flowery marketing language and buzz words. Of course, your game is unique, fun, and highly replayable, but everyone says the same thing about their game.

Aim to include the seven key elements above, including some great visuals to get publishers excited, and your sell sheet will do the selling for you.

Check out some great examples of successful sell sheets in the bonus section at tinyurl.com/bgbonuspage.

## Take Action

I want you to **write down details for the seven key elements for your game**. Now use these details to develop the first draft of your sell sheet. Don't worry if it doesn't look perfect. The goal is to have something you can use. Then, you can improve upon this and make it look better. You just need to get started

# 11

# How to Avoid Overdoing Your Overview Video

> The best thing to send me: An under 3-minute video explaining the game. Nothing helps me make a go or no-go decision faster than seeing a game in action.
>
> **– Adam McCrimmon, XYZ Game Labs**

Your game's all set up on the table. Check. Lighting's just right. Check. Camera on. Check.

Now, what the heck are you supposed to say?

How are you going to get a publisher to watch this video of your game all the way through without falling asleep?

In the last chapter we walked through all the steps you need to create a compelling sell sheet, and now we'll move forward with your next step: the overview video.

While your sell sheet is a good visual representation of your game, many publishers will also request an overview video or pitch video of your game as well.

This video will go a little more in-depth into your game, allowing you to demonstrate exactly what the game looks like and how it's played.

Many designers creating their first overview video make one big mistake. That one mistake can cost them the opportunity to work with that publisher.

I don't want you to make this common pitfall, so keep reading.

DOI: 10.1201/9781003334828-14

## What You Need to Include

So, how do you create a great overview video and ensure a publisher is going to be hanging on every word?

Here are the main elements you want to include in your video:

- The name of your game and your own name as the designer
- The player count and approximate length of the game
- What the game is about and what players do (remember that 30-second elevator pitch you put together? Here's another place where this will come in handy).
- A walkthrough of your game, demonstrating what a player can do on their turn

One other thing I included in a recent overview video, which a publisher really appreciated and was likely one of the main reasons they inquired about it further and ended up signing the game, was that I showed some *actual gameplay*.

It is a quick bluffing game that really needs to be seen in action to get a good feel for the game. So, my wife and I recorded a playthrough of a full game, which was only about 10 minutes. Then I watched the whole video over and kept only a short segment that really demonstrated the game and how much fun it was to play. It felt natural and really highlighted the bluffing and chaining together of cards that players can do.

This was submitted to a contest, and one judge, who also happened to be a publisher, said it was the only video submitted to the contest he saw which had actual gameplay included. He rated my video five stars across the board, and they ended up signing and publishing the game, which is called *Zoo Year's Eve*.

If you can include a short segment of gameplay in your overview video, I would highly recommend this.

## What You Want to Leave Out

Remember that mistake I mentioned that many new game designers make? Well here it is in four short words:

Explaining. Every. Single. Rule.

The purpose of an overview video is to get a publisher's attention and have them wanting more. You want the publisher to watch your video and then either ask to set up a meeting for a demo or request your prototype.

Remember, you're not teaching the game to new players. Yes, you want to explain what players can do, but you don't have to get into the nitty-gritty details of every single rule in your game.

It doesn't have to be fancy or professionally made. It should not be all marketing and hype.

You can record this with a camera that can capture video or even use your phone if the picture quality is pretty decent.

But I caution you *not to use the internal mic*. The sound is often not that great, and you want to make sure that the listener will be hanging on every word. Test the mic on your phone or camera first to see how clear the audio is, especially when you move around the table explaining your game. Unless it is really clear, consider using a better mic.

If you don't have a decent mic, pick one up. They're not that expensive, and a good mic is a great investment. Look for a lapel or lavalier mic you can clip onto your shirt, with a good length of cord. This should give you clean, clear audio and allow you to move around and have your voice captured consistently.

## Keep It to a Good Length

When you're recording your overview video, be sure to keep it to a reasonable length.

Under 5 minutes is what you're aiming for. Keeping it to 2–3 minutes if possible is even better.

Some publishers or contests have more stringent timelines, so you may have to explain your entire game in as little as 2 minutes. This is where you can use that 2-minute pitch while having the game on camera so that you can demonstrate all the actions while you talk.

Be concise and to the point. Avoid rambling or going into too much detail.

## Emphasize What Makes Your Game Different

In terms of emphasis, focus on the most interesting aspect of your game, particularly what is unique about your game.

Think about what makes your game stand out from other games, and why someone would want to play your game over another.

Is there an interesting mechanic that's never been used before, or at least not in the way that you've implemented?

Is your game super thematic in a way you've never seen done before? Think about the hook. What makes your game stand out?

Make sure to also emphasize your game's uniqueness in your overview video.

If you can get it all down in one take, you can avoid having to do any editing (or at least keep it to a minimum). But, don't worry if you have to do a little editing. There are plenty of free or inexpensive options for editing software, like Hitfilm Express, Apple iMovie, Blender, and Lightworks. I use Microsoft Movie Maker. It's not fancy, but it's easy to use and came with my computer, so I'm familiar with it and there was no additional cost to me. Like most things, the best software is the one that you'll use.

I've made several overview videos for contests and pitching to publishers. Some have been good, and some have been bad.

But with each video, I've improved. I now use the techniques outlined in this chapter to demonstrate exactly what publishers want to see, and this has helped me to get multiple prototype requests and games signed with publishers.

Check out an example of the very simple overview video I recorded for *Zoo Year's Eve* that had my future publisher immediately say, "I want to sign this game" in the bonus section at tinyurl.com/bgbonuspage.

## Take Action

Set your game up on the table. Next, set up your phone or camera and hit record. Talk about your game – what it's about, what players do, what a turn looks like, and what makes it unique. This is just a practice video so that you can get more comfortable and hone your skills, so don't worry about making mistakes!

Then, when you've got it down, record your video again. If you have to shoot multiple takes, that's ok. I rarely get it right on the first try!

# 12

# Putting Together Everything Else You'll Need

> Try to create an idea or brand for yourself, in order to make it easier for them to remember you.
>
> **– Don Eskridge**

Now, let's go over everything else you'll need before you start pitching your game to publishers.

## Rulebook

We already covered rulebooks in Chapter 5, so I won't go into it much further here.

Suffice to say, make sure your rulebook is up-to-date, with plenty of images and examples, and has been thoroughly reviewed and tested to ensure that a publisher will be able to easily understand your game and play it right the first time.

It would be a huge disappointment to have a potential publisher reject your game without even playing it because they couldn't figure out how to play it or got a crucial rule wrong. You've made a great game, now make sure that they can understand how to play!

## Working Prototype

It goes without saying that you need to have a functioning prototype to demo your game and hand it over to a publisher once this is requested.

DOI: 10.1201/9781003334828-15

So, I'll just mention ensuring that everything they will need to play your game is included in the box. Take everything out and try to set up your game. Is everything there that you need? Are any cubes or tokens missing?

Make sure to include all components, your rules, and your contact information (in multiple places—sticker on the front or back of the box top, on your rules, etc.). I've had prototypes go missing, which is never fun to hear about. Labeling it with your name greatly increases your chances of getting it back!

It's also great to have multiple copies of your game if possible. That way, you're ready in case more than one publisher wants to take it home to evaluate further. Just make sure publishers know that others are looking at it as well!

**Pro tip:** If you're handing over a prototype to a publisher at a convention, it's often easier if you put everything into a Ziploc style bag. This way it takes up less valuable luggage space and is lighter to transport (for both you and the publisher). Just make sure it is well-labeled!

## Print and Play Files

If your game isn't overly complex and doesn't have too many components (or at least uses fairly common components like six-sided dice and meeples), it can be helpful to have a print and play (PnP) file readily available. If your game only uses a small number of cards and other components, it may not be too much effort for another person to print out and put a copy of your game together.

Your PnP will often be in the form of a PDF, which includes everything a player will need to print out and play your game. Just make sure to mention any additional components (and quantities of these) that a player will need to supply for themselves.

These PnP files are handy to provide to publishers who live far from you as well as to reduce the time and cost of shipping prototypes back and forth. They can also be very useful to give to other players outside your region to playtest.

## Business Cards

It can also be helpful to have business cards handy. They are quick to make and cheap to order in large quantities.

When you have a business card with you at Cons and other events, you have a way to keep in touch with other designers you meet, as well as to give to publishers, or to include as contact information with your prototype. Just drop one into the box or staple it to your rulebook.

There are only a few main things you really need to include:

- Your name
- Your company name and logo (if applicable)
- Your email address
- Your phone number

You can optionally include other information such as your website and social media accounts, but make sure to at least cover the basics above.

## Digital Version of Your Game (Optional)

Take to the Internet!

If you live somewhere remote, are having trouble finding other gamers and game designers in your area, or are just a bit on the shy side, have no fear! Even though tabletop games are typically played face-to-face, there are ways to create and test your game digitally.

Two of the most well-known tools are Tabletop Simulator (tabletopsimulator.com) and Tabletopia (tabletopia.com).

These sites allow you to create your game and play with others online. This is not only great for playing games with others, but also for designing a game remotely with a co-designer. You can even join Facebook groups dedicated to digital tabletop game playtesting.

## Take Action

Make sure you have your rules, a functioning prototype, and print and play files ready.

Also, check out Tabletop Simulator (tabletopsimulator.com) and Tabletopia (tabletopia.com) to see if either one is right for you.

# Section III

# How to Find the Right Publisher

# 13

# First, Figure Out Who Is Going to Want Your Game

> I've seen and played a LOT of games, and especially now with so many new games coming out, a pitch has to really excite me before I get too interested.
>
> **– Seth Jaffee, Tasty Minstrel Games**

Ok, you've got a game that's amazing and everyone wants to buy it. You've put together a well-written set of rules that have been blind play-tested, and you've worked out all the kinks.

Your pitch, sell sheet, and overview video are top-notch.

Now all you have to do is hand it over to a publisher and you're done, right? Well, not exactly.

Not every publisher is going to be a great match for your game. Nor do you want to just hand your game over to the first one who shows interest.

If you start submitting your game to every publisher on Earth, you're going to be met with a lot of disappointment. Not to mention wrecking any chance of getting your future games in front of them.

What you need to do now is create a list of potential publishers who would be a good match for your game.

## Think Like Edison

I'm going to share with you one of the best resources I've ever found.

I once started to create a resource much like this on my own, but after researching and listing out all the info I could find on about 40 publishers,

DOI: 10.1201/9781003334828-17

I realized how much work it would be to keep this list (which was nowhere near complete yet) up-to-date.

That's when I discovered the Cardboard Edison Compendium (tinyurl.com/cardboardedison).

This super-helpful compendium is a list of well over 240 publishers (yes, 240 publishers!) and counting, including the types of games they're looking for, how they prefer to be contacted, if they are currently accepting submissions, and their contact information. Even better, the publishers have filled out all the information themselves, so you know it's legit.

It's well worth the tiny investment (which can either be done as a small one-time fee to access all this information forever or as a small monthly Patreon pledge) to get your hands on this wealth of information. Think about how many hours you will save not having to compile such a list yourself!

## Another Amazing Resource

If you're looking to reach the right publishers, it all starts with research. You're learning the process of how to research, but maybe you don't have time to research the hundreds of publishers out there.

Tabletoppublishers.com offers the most comprehensive database of publishers in the tabletop industry. It's the most extensive collection of publishers available and is updated on a regular basis. It's also filterable in many different ways to help you to find a perfect fit between your game and potential publishers.

This resource is provided by Chris Backe of Entro Games. It is based on the same information he has laboriously researched for his own games, and he has expanded on it to create an industry-leading tool.

Rather hand off the research altogether? Chris also offers a do-the-research-for-you service. Fill in a form on the website, sharing the details of your game, and in a few business days, he'll respond with a carefully-curated list of the best fits. See the website for costs and how it all works.

## Look for Similarities

Another great way to create your list of preferred publishers is to look at the games on your shelf, your local game store, or online to find similar titles.

If there's a publisher you love who is putting out great games that are similar to yours and has been successful with this approach, you might want to include them on your shortlist.

You'll be looking for publishers with a similar audience who would make a great match for you and your game.

## Match Publishers to Your Game

Now that you have a compiled list of potential publishers, have a good look through their catalog of games.

Do they have any games that are somewhat similar to yours? Are any of their games almost exactly like your game?

If your game is too much like one of theirs, they will see your game as a competing product. Make sure your game complements, not competes. If your game is too close to one of theirs, you're better off approaching other publishers.

However, if your game is only similar in terms of style (complexity, audience, and similar theme, for example), then your game may complement their existing catalog of games. This is really what you're looking for—a game that can sit right beside their other games, but still feel unique.

## Narrow Down and Rank Your List

You've probably now got a reasonably good list of potential publishers you can approach. But you don't necessarily want to try a shotgun approach where you send it to 20 or 30 publishers all at the same time.

What you want to do is narrow down your list to publishers you'd most like to work with (who of course you've already identified as a potential match).

## Prioritize

Now, rank your top 5 to 10 publishers. This will be the order in which you contact them.

Start with your most ideal publisher. Think about why you chose them as your number one.

Is it because they sell a lot of copies of their games? Do they make some of your favorite games?

Have you heard they're great to work with? Determine what's most important to you.

If you have more than 10 potential publishers on your list, you can always consider approaching them next if your top choices take a pass.

## Take Action

I want you to **go check out the** Cardboard Edison Compendium (tinyurl.com/cardboardedison) and Tabletoppublishers.com. Invest a few bucks in one of these highly worthwhile resources and start scanning through and making a list of potential publishers who would be a good match for your game. Narrow this further to the top 5 to 10 best matches for your game. Check out the submission pages for each of these publishers and make sure to bookmark these pages for easy access later.

# 14

# How to Get Meetings at Conventions (Cons)

> This is very much an industry of connections. Who you know is often as important as what you've made and going to conventions is the best way to build those relationships with fellow designers and potential publishers.
>
> – **Eric Slauson**

Conventions (Cons) are a busy time for publishers. They are often focused on releasing and demoing new games, and likely won't have a lot of time to talk to you about your brilliant game idea. Unless of course, you make arrangements in advance.

Cons present a great opportunity to meet with a number of publishers all in one trip. If you can get some dedicated time with a publisher, this will be your chance to demo a game in front of them and start to build a relationship.

## Plan Ahead

It's much better to contact these publishers ahead of time, usually at least a month in advance, to pitch them your game via a sell sheet and/or overview video. Then, if they are interested, you can arrange to meet so that you can show them your game during a pre-arranged time rather than just showing up at their booth and making a pitch.

You'll find that contacting these publishers is very hit-and-miss. You'll reach out to them, provide a sell sheet, along with a brief description of why

DOI: 10.1201/9781003334828-18

you think the game is a good fit for them, and may never hear back. Other publishers may get back to you and let you know that they are either not currently accepting submissions or that your game doesn't quite match what they are looking for right now. However, you might just find that one publisher who would be quite interested to set up a meeting with you.

If you're able to arrange something, make sure to confirm how much time you have for the meeting. But, also be prepared in case they have less time than originally expected. Things come up and a publisher may be stretched for time.

## Be Prepared

Practice your pitch and make it concise. Give them an overview of how the game is played, and if time permits, you may be able to play a round or two of the game so that they can see exactly how it works.

If you have multiple games (which I strongly recommend once you get some experience in game design), make sure to have these with you. If a publisher isn't interested in the game you're pitching or they already have a game in their queue that is similar, you always want to have a backup plan. Ask them what they're looking for. Show them something else that might pique their interest. Sometimes it's just a numbers game. Having multiple games to pitch is always a wise idea.

## Getting the Most Bang for Your Buck

It's also important to be selective about which Cons you are attending if you intend to pitch your game to publishers.

While Gen Con and Essen are the biggest conventions, they are not necessarily the best places to meet with publishers. Often there are hundreds of new games being released at these major Cons, so publishers are quite busy introducing, demoing, and selling their games.

Consequently, if you go to some very small Cons, there may not be any publishers there at all. These may just be small events where locals get together and play games.

The sweet spot is often found in the medium to large (but not huge) Cons. You'll want to look for Cons where many publishers will be attending and hopefully also where there will be a publisher/designer speed dating event as well.

## My Recommendations

My top pick, which is also favored by many other game designers, is the **Origins Game Fair**. This is considered a large Con by most standards, yet it is not nearly as crazy as Gen Con or Essen. If you can only get to one Con to pitch your game, Origins might just be your best bet.

However, I recently attended my first **PAX Unplugged** and had quite a bit of success there. The upside to this convention is that it is held late in the year, at the end of "Con Season." Publishers are slowing down a bit and will likely have more time to look at and play prototypes following this event.

Yes, publishers will be there releasing new games, but not nearly at the same volume as the biggest conventions. It is a slightly more relaxed atmosphere, and with publishers being not quite as busy, there are more opportunities to meet with them. Also, Origins runs for five full days, so publishers may have a bit more time in their schedule than they would at other smaller Cons.

You may want to consider some smaller Cons and events where there is a decent list of publishers attending. You may even want to check out one of the toy fairs in Chicago and New York, although they are harder to get into without the right connections.

Here is a link to a site showing most of the tabletop events out there, along with a helpful map so that you can see what is happening where and when.

https://casualgamerevolution.com/

When you go to the site, just click on "**Conventions**" for a map and a full list of Conventions happening for the current year.

**Be warned:** There is quite a long list of events here and some are focused more on playtesting or straight-up gaming, so they might not be the best places to pitch your game (some may have few publishers, if any, attending)!

## Here Are Some Tips to Increase Your Chances of Getting a Meeting Set Up With a Publisher

Have your sell sheets, overview videos, rules, and prototypes ready before you contact anyone.

As always, make sure your game plays really well and is a good match for the publisher.

Contact publishers 1–2 months before the Con or event to see if they have any interest in your game and if so, set up a meeting.

When you reach out to a publisher, make it personal. Rather than sending a generic email, mention some of their games that you enjoy and why you feel your game would be a good fit for them.

Schedule a specific time and meeting location with the publisher, away from the busyness if possible, to make it easier to focus.

When booking your meeting, the earlier in the duration of the event, the better. Most publishers will be tired after the end of the long day in the vendor hall.

Practice setting up and tearing down your game(s) quickly. If you can be there early and set up in advance, even better.

Prepare your pitch, along with how to quickly set up and demo your game (publishers are busy folks and may even have to cut back their meeting time with you).

Keep these tips in mind, and you'll increase your chances of meeting with that publisher you've been eyeing.

## Take Action

Check out what Cons and other board gaming events are coming up in the year. If you're able to take some time off and travel a bit, make a list of the top events you'd like to attend. You may not be able to get to all of them, but this will give you a list to work from. If you can't travel far, determine which events are happening close to home that might have some publishers attending.

Aim to have your game(s) ready and in good shape for when you're planning to attend the next event.

# 15

# How to Wow Publishers at a Speed Dating Event

> Never give up. If you are persistent, (and you don't suck) and you want it bad enough, you will eventually get published.
>
> **– Scott Rogers**

Quite often at larger Cons, there will be an event dedicated to designers pitching their games to publishers, known as a publisher speed dating event (or speed pitching event). When you hear about these events or are planning on attending one of these conventions, sign up early, because spots are extremely limited, and the tickets sell out very quickly.

## How Speed Dating Events Work

Depending on the event, you may just need to sign up, or you may be required to submit a sell sheet and/or other info on your game. In the latter case, there may be a judging competition to select games that will be considered for the event.

If you get a seat at the event, you'll be given space to set up your game, display your sell sheet, and set out your business cards if you have any (it's always a good idea to have some). You will have a short amount of time, typically around 3–5 minutes, to pitch your game and answer any questions.

Unless your game is really simple to teach and get into, in which case you might be able to demo a sample round of the game, focus on what players do in your game, the experience they will have, and what is unique about your game.

DOI: 10.1201/9781003334828-19

Publishers will dive deeper with questions if they are interested. Make sure to thank them for their time and exchange business cards if you're able to.

If the publisher likes what they see, they will likely take a sell sheet, which may or may not indicate a strong interest in your game. If they want to play your game or find out more information, they will reach out to you (possibly while you're still at the convention or event) with the contact information you've provided.

## There's Power in Numbers

These speed dating events can be hit or miss. If they are not well-attended by reputable publishers, the odds of gaining interest or getting your game signed as a result of attending can diminish.

On the other hand, all it takes is one interested publisher to get a game signed. The big benefit of these events is they allow you to show your game to multiple publishers in a very short amount of time. You can also get business cards and start to develop a relationship with lots of publishers. This can make it easier when you have other games you'd like to pitch to them at a later date.

I made the mistake of setting up five games I was working on at my first-speed dating event. Although I got quite good at giving a 15-second run-down of each game, it was probably a bit much for any publisher to take in. So, focus on one game. If a publisher happens to mention something else they're looking for that meets the criteria for another game you have with you, mention this to them, and ask if they'd like to take a sell sheet for this or meet afterward to discuss the other game.

Pitching your game over and over can be a bit stressful if you're not used to it. However, you will definitely get better at pitching your game the more you do it, so this is great practice.

Here are some tips to improve your odds at speed dating events:

- Sign up as soon as you can, as there are always a limited number of spots and way more demand than supply.
- This may go without saying but have a great looking and great playing game to pitch. Quite often, many of the games presented at these events are not top-notch (at least not yet), so having a really good-looking prototype that also plays well can help a lot.
- Get there early and have everything set up well before the publishers arrive.

- Practice your pitch ahead of time and have it down cold (a 30-second elevator pitch outlining the game and what players do is a great starting point—remember this from the earlier chapter?).
- Have plenty of copies of your sell sheet (and business cards if you have these) and make sure to display your sell sheet on a standee to stand out.
- Make sure to get the names of the representatives you talk to and ask for a business card from each of the publishers you meet.
- Be polite and professional, and show the publishers that you are somebody they would want to work with.

Remember, just because a publisher is interested, doesn't mean you need to sign with them, or even hand over your prototype (they will not hand you a contract right then and there anyways). Make sure you get to know the publisher. It's similar to a job interview. You both have to feel this is a good fit. It's ok to say no or ask for some time to think it over.

## Take Action

If you're planning on attending a Con or other event, check to see if there is a speed dating event planned. Keep checking in to see when registration is open and get your submission in as early as you can if required. Since you'll already have your pitch and sell sheet ready, this should be an easy process for you.

# 16

# Going to Cons Without Going Broke

> You cannot predict exactly what a publisher is looking for. So, make sure that they see your game.
>
> – **Asger Harding Granerud**

I've seen a lot of posts in forums and groups talking about how difficult it is for game designers to get to conventions (Cons) and whether they are worth it, so I thought it would be helpful to share some thoughts on this with you here from my experience and through learning from others.

## The Value of Meeting Others in Person

The truth is you will definitely improve the odds of getting your game signed with a publisher considerably if you can meet with them in person. There are many reasons for this, including the ability to develop a stronger relationship through face-to-face communication and being able to demo the game and answer questions in real time. It's not crucial, and I have had games signed by publishers whom I didn't meet at Cons (and in fact, in some cases have never even met in person!), but it certainly can often help.

Even if the game you're pitching isn't a good match for them, you can still get business cards and contact information so you can more easily reach out to these publishers with future games. They may even mention another publisher to you who would be a better fit.

DOI: 10.1201/9781003334828-20

If you want to be a game designer, you'll definitely need to make more than one game in your lifetime. Your first game will also likely not be your best. It may never get published. So, having these connections can be very helpful. This makes it much easier than cold emailing a generic "info" or "support" mailbox.

Now having said that, it can be expensive to travel to these events, and the costs could definitely outweigh any potential revenue you could receive from your games (at least right away).

## Be Selective

The best approach is to pick just one or two Cons to go to and make the most of your time there. You don't have to attend every one of them. Pick an event where there will be a lot of publishers present, particularly ones that would be a good match for your game, and where they will not be crazy busy.

GenCon and Essen are usually the busiest times for publishers, as they are releasing some of their biggest games of the year. Other conventions, such as Origins and PAX Unplugged, are a much better option.

Also, if you can get a seat in a publisher speed dating event, this is a great opportunity to meet many publishers within a very short time.

Pitching more than one game while at a Con can make it more efficient as well. As long as your games are good and well playtested, you stand a higher chance of getting one signed if you have multiple games you're pitching to multiple publishers.

Many publishers prefer to meet at these events because they are already there, and this gives them the chance to get to know both the designer and their game more intimately. Getting a publisher's undivided attention can go a long way compared to waiting for them to reply to you or eventually try out the prototype you sent them.

## Other Benefits and Considerations

Conventions are also a great place to try out new games, meet new people, and just have fun. However, it's definitely worthwhile to set aside some dedicated time to meet with publishers. If this is a 3–5- day event, you'll also have the opportunity to do whatever you like the rest of the time (playtesting, playing games, sitting in on demos, etc.).

If conventions are not a possibility for you, due to costs, physical constraints, anxiety, or perhaps where you're located, you could also consider asking another designer you know and trust who is also familiar with your game(s) if they would be willing to pitch your game to publishers. If you go this route, make it worthwhile for anyone who is helping you. Offer to cover some of their Con expenses or share a portion of the royalties as if they were acting as an agent for you (more on this later in the book).

The ticket price for Cons is negligible compared to other costs you may incur. Your biggest expenses will likely be accommodations and transportation. Food will likely be next, followed by the cost of the badge. You may also spend money on additional tickets for speed dating/pitching events, talks, or other events. If you buy any games while you're there, well, that's another cost, but one of a personal nature.

Here are some tips to keep costs down and ensure that going to Cons and other events are more worthwhile:

### *Schedule Your Meetings in Advance*

Make the most of both your time and a publisher's time by scheduling a meeting about 1–2 months before the event rather than pitching to them when they're busy at their booth. You can also try to book all your meetings within a day or two if possible if you don't want to stay for the duration of the event. Also, if you can schedule those meetings on an earlier day during the Con as opposed to near the end, the publisher will likely have more energy and enthusiasm, as running a booth for multiple days can be exhausting!

### *Speed Dating*

Attend a speed dating event if one is offered. This is your opportunity to put your game in front of a number of publishers over an hour or two.

### *Travel With Others*

If you can drive or otherwise travel to the event with others, you can save money by splitting gas, accommodations, and any other expenses. This is also a great time to brainstorm and potentially collaborate on game ideas with others. You can develop some great friendships and relationships, which is especially welcome when you are doing the somewhat solitary job of designing games.

### *Phone a Friend*

If you know someone who lives in the area where the Con is being held, see if you can stay with them. By staying in their spare room or couch-surfing for a few nights, you can save a lot of money.

### *Stay Close By*

Most events happen at or near a hotel. If there are spots still available, you may be able to stay there or somewhere nearby to save yourself time, however, the trade-off is that it will be more costly. It's a balance of time and money. Book early to get the best selection and prices.

### *Alternative Accommodations*

Another alternative is to look for places to stay through Airbnb. Even just booking a room as opposed to a whole suite or home can save you a lot of money, especially if the only time you'll be there is to sleep.

### *Eat Smart*

Pack some of your own meals and snacks to save you time and money, and to allow you to eat healthier if you choose.

### *Volunteer and Make Connections*

One great way to both save money and make more connections is through volunteering.

Contact publishers to see if they need any volunteers to help with demoing games or anything else at their booth. Many will cover the cost of your badge and maybe even part of your accommodations. If you can spare some time to help a publisher, this cannot only save you money but also allow you to get to know them, which could make it easier to pitch a game to them in the future. After all, if someone lent you a hand, wouldn't you be more eager to help them out?

### *Go Local*

Look for local events. The closer these are to home, the less you'll have to spend.

By combining a number of the options above, you can attend Cons with relatively little money out of pocket, so long as you aren't traveling halfway around the world to attend.

If you're not able or not interested in going to these events, there are some alternatives, including pitching through email, referrals, using an agent, or entering game design contests.

## Take Action

If you're planning on attending a Con or other event, check well in advance to see if others you know are also attending. Reach out to publishers to see if they are looking for volunteers to demo games. Plan your accommodations in advance. Schedule as many meetings as you can and have your games ready to pitch. Make sure you don't blow all your dough on one event!

# 17

# Reaching Out to Publishers

> It is quite a complex mix. The most important though is do I have a clear vision of a product after my first contact with the game.
>
> **– Filip Milunski, Lucky Duck Games**

Quite often, the first contact you will have with a publisher is through email (or perhaps a form on their website). This is often the only way, other than showing up at their booth without an invitation, to get in touch with a publisher.

So, let's look at how you can start off on the right foot to turn an inquiry email into an interested publisher.

## Referrals

One great way to find out about and make connections with suitable publishers is through referrals. If you know other game designers or have friends in the industry, they may be able to put you in touch with a publisher that would be a good fit for your game.

A good friend or colleague will also be honest about who is good to work with, and who you might be better off avoiding. Remember that it's not just you looking for a publisher, the publisher is also looking for great games and easy-to-work-with designers.

Think of this as a job interview. Sure, you might want to get your game published really badly, but it's not worth partnering with someone who won't be a good fit and won't work with you in the way you would have hoped.

DOI: 10.1201/9781003334828-21

It's better to first find good possible matches, talk to them, and figure out if this publisher is someone you'd want to work with. It's ok to say no or keep looking. There are plenty of publishers out there, big and small, with different desires and ideas of how to run their businesses.

I've been very fortunate myself to make connections and get referrals. I found out about a local publisher, who at first, I thought was just a designer but turned out to also be looking for games like the ones I was creating. I've also been given contacts for larger companies that were starting to branch out into board games, giving me an early advantage. All this came simply through talking with other designers, offering helpful feedback, and generally being nice to others.

The first game I ever signed with a publisher, a co-designed word game called *Four Word Thinking*, was through a referral. Another designer tried my game at a convention and thought it would be a good fit for the publisher he had recently signed a game with. He gave us their direct contact information (much better than a generic "submissions@" email address). When I reached out to them, I mentioned that the other designer recommended we contact them, and the rest, as they say, is history.

Here are some tips for getting referrals:

- Build relationships with other game designers.
- Be helpful to others and let the law of reciprocity take action.
- Ask other designers if they know a publisher who would be a good fit for your game (just don't be too pushy about this, as they may just not know someone who would be a good match).
- Talk to other designers that the publishers have worked with, and about their experience with these publishers.
- If you discover a publisher who may be a good match for you, try to find a specific contact, as this will allow you to better personalize your communications.
- Ask the person who is providing the referral if you can mention their name. This can be helpful, as they will see you in a better light if they have a good working relationship with the person who referred you.
- Give a very brief intro to your game using your elevator pitch. You may wish to include your sell sheet as well.
- As always, have your sell sheets, overview videos, rules, and prototypes ready when you contact a publisher.

## Cold Emails

I know that emailing publishers with whom you don't have existing relationships can seem daunting. I've reached out to dozens of publishers myself and have had successes, passes, and more than anything else, a LOT of non-responses.

Publishers are busy. They have hundreds, if not thousands, of people contacting them every year with their latest and greatest game idea. Some publishers accept outside submissions and others do not so make sure to do your homework.

Most publishers will clearly state on their website whether or not they are accepting submissions, which will save you some time and effort, as you can focus on only reaching out to those currently looking for games. You don't want to waste your time or theirs by pitching a game when they are not even looking at submissions.

Also, make sure that the game or games you're pitching are a good match for the publisher. There should be some similarity to their existing games, but not so comparable that your game would be competing directly with games already in their catalog.

When you do contact a publisher, make sure to follow any process they've outlined. They may indicate that you must fill out a form or that you only provide certain information. Generally, it's best to email them, introducing yourself and why you feel your game is a good match for them. Avoid generic emails and make sure to personalize your message to them. Nobody enjoys receiving a standard generic email that is clearly being sent to many others with the exact same message. This will greatly increase your chances of receiving a reply.

Don't just send publishers a prototype of your game or a print and play file when you first contact them. Simply include a brief description of the game, including the hook and why it would be a good match for them.

Also include your sell sheet, outlining important aspects of your game as well as your contact information. If they're interested, they may ask you to send the rules or a short playthrough video to demonstrate how the game is played. It's not a bad idea to have both of these ready in advance, to keep the conversation moving forward and keep yourself at the front of the publisher's mind.

Don't be discouraged if you don't hear back. Some publishers aren't looking for games at the moment. Others may just be inundated with emails and can't reply to each one promptly. Feel free to send a follow-up email a couple of weeks later. Perhaps the publisher had meant to reply or look at your email again, and this will jog their memory. In other cases, you just may not hear back. Sometimes that's just the way it is.

To summarize, here are some tips to increase your chances of getting a response when you send a cold email to a publisher:

- Make sure to check the publisher's website to determine if they are accepting outside submissions, and if so, what their procedure and requirements are.
- Only reach out to publishers who are currently accepting submissions and make sure to follow their procedures. Failure to do so shows the publisher that you can't follow instructions and will likely result in your submission being ignored.
- Personalize your message. Don't just send a generic form letter. Mention some of their games that you enjoy and why you feel your game would be a good fit for them.
- Give a very brief intro to your game using your elevator pitch. You will want to include your sell sheet as well.
- In addition to your sell sheets, have your overview videos, rules, and prototypes ready when you contact them, in case they want to know more about your game.
- If you don't hear anything back, follow-up in two weeks. Remember that publishers are busy and receive tons of pitches. They may just not have gotten to yours yet.

For email templates you can use based on emails I've sent publishers to set up meetings and get strong interest, make sure to check out the bonus section for this book at tinyurl.com/bgbonuspage.

## Take Action

Go to the website of the top publisher on your list and look up their submission process. If they are accepting submissions and have a contact email address for this, write an email to them using the template in the bonus section mentioned above and then personalize your message for that publisher. Let them know what's so special about your game, why they'd want to publish it, and why you want to work with them. If they use a submission form, fill this out to the best of your ability, making use of your elevator pitch. In either case, make sure to include your sell sheet and a link to your video.

# 18

# Why You Need to Enter Game Design Contests

> Many of the competitions around the world are judged by publishers or other designers, and some can even lead to a contract. Two of my games found publishers through this pathway.
>
> **– Phil Walker-Harding**

Many game design contests happen throughout the year. Some are looking for specific games, such as social deduction, 2-player, or solo games, whereas other contests are open to any type of game submission.

There is usually a small cost involved in submitting your game to one of these contests. Occasionally they will be free (mostly contests on boardgamegeek.com), but many will charge around $5–$20 or more per entry.

Is it worth the cost?

In my opinion, the answer is a resounding **yes**.

But not necessarily for all the reasons, you may be thinking. Yes, some of these contests do give out prizes such as gift cards for retail games and game design-related websites, however, this is one of the last things I think of when it comes to game design contests.

## The Best Reason to Enter a Game Design Contest

The number one reason I enter game design contests is for **critical feedback**. Many of these contests are judged by game design professionals who know their stuff. Whether you advance to the next round or not, you'll get written

DOI: 10.1201/9781003334828-22

feedback from multiple judges, which can be really helpful to improve your game and understand the next steps to take.

There's also the possibility that your game may be seen by an interested publisher, especially if your game makes it to the final round of judging (which may be limited to 5–10 or perhaps more submissions depending on the contest), as more eyes will be on it at every stage. A number of the judges will actually be game publishers, and one of the reasons they judge these contests is that they might just find their next game. So, by entering a really solid game into one of these contests, you could find a publisher who is interested in pursuing this further. Even if you don't win, one of these publishers may ask you if they can take the prototype home for further evaluation, and you never know, they may end up wanting to sign your game.

I entered two of my games in a contest called the Board Game Design Lab Design Challenge, and although neither even made it out of the first round, amazing things happened to both of the games I submitted. The two games I entered were *Isle of Rock n Roll*, a game where you play as a band competing for world domination on the rock stage, and *Zoo Year's Eve*, a fast-paced bluffing game about sneaking your team of animals out of the zoo (this was later changed to sneaking your animals into a party).

I wasn't setting out to win the contest (although I wouldn't have complained if either game had won). My goal was to get GOOD QUALITY FEEDBACK on my games. As I mentioned, that is the biggest reason, in my opinion, why you want to enter your game into any contest. The feedback I received was more than worth the small entry fee, and although some of it was critical, it was extremely helpful.

In the case of *Isle of Rock n Roll*, the two judges had completely different impressions of the game. Even worse, neither of these impressions were reflective of the actual game. This wasn't either of the judge's faults. This was on me. I didn't clearly convey what the game was about.

The important thing is what I did with this feedback. I was planning on showcasing *Isle of Rock n Roll* at the upcoming Origins publisher speed dating event in a matter of weeks, so I used this feedback to improve my sell sheet and tighten up my pitch.

The result? Not one, but THREE publishers took a strong interest in *Isle of Rock n Roll*. So, even if the first publisher takes a pass, I have a backup plan with an additional backup plan in place.

## The Other Really Good Reason to Enter a Contest

The second reason I mentioned you want to enter game design contests is EXPOSURE. Remember, some of the judges are publishers as well.

Fortunately for me, *Zoo Year's Eve* landed in front of a publisher who loved the game and wanted to see more. That publisher was Adam McCrimmon of XYZ Game Labs. So, I took it to Origins to show it to Adam and his team. They immediately fell in love with the game and took a prototype right on the spot.

Fast forward a few months and we signed the contract for *Zoo Year's Eve*. It became my first published game despite it being the third contract I signed, as my publisher was eager to release it at an upcoming Con and knew they could move fast on this since it was a small game that was easy to produce.

So, if you're hesitant to enter a game design contest, remember: The feedback and exposure to publishers you receive can be more than worth the time and effort. If you win, great! But that's just the icing on the cake.

And if you win one of these contests or at least place highly, this probably won't hurt your chances of getting your game published in the future either. You can let publishers know where it placed in certain contests when you are discussing the game with them. This could be included in your sell sheet, an email, or when discussing your game in person. If you decide to self-publish this game later, any award you can mention would be an additional selling point.

So, you can see that this very small investment could be very beneficial, even if your game doesn't advance to the next round. At the very least, you will get some professional feedback on your game.

## Why Contests Will Make You a Better Designer

A game design contest may require you to work within some kind of constraints. It might be creating a game with only 18 cards (Buttonshy), using only specific components (Haba), or another restriction.

This will make you think differently and work within a smaller set of parameters. You'll no longer have anything you want at your disposal. Restrictions can actually make a game much better.

The other thing a contest does is give you focus. You only have a limited time to create and playtest your game, as you are working toward a deadline. No more "I'll work on my game when inspiration hits me". No. You'll have to get your game running smoothly in a very short amount of time, quite often in only one to three months.

These deadlines will help you to get better at game design quickly. But where do you find these contests?

Well, there are a number of them running throughout the year.

If you subscribe to the Board Game Design Lab email list (which I highly recommend), you will receive an email every week with links to a bunch of great game design resources, a new podcast episode, and a list of current game contests. Here (boardgamedesignlab.com) is a link to the Board Game Design Lab site where you can sign up for the mailing list.

## Where to Find Game Design Contests

There's also a list of upcoming contests available here (cardboardedison.com/contests) at Cardboard Edison.

Here are some of the sites that offer game design contests throughout the year (be on the lookout for others as well):

- Boardgamegeek.com (multiple specific contests running throughout the year)
- The Board Game Design Lab (boardgamedesignlab.com)
- The Board Game Workshop (theboardgameworkshop.com)
- Cardboard Edison (cardboardedison.com)
- The Gamecrafter (thegamecrafter.com)
- Haba (www.habausa.com/) (children's game contest where they ship you a box of components to use)
- Hippodice (hippodice-competition.net)

The requirements for these game contests vary. Those on boardgamegeek.com rely more on members to vote on them, and usually require a print and play version of your game.

Many of the other contests require a sell sheet and perhaps a playthrough video for the first round. If you advance, you may be asked to submit rules and/or a prototype for evaluation.

Overall, the feedback alone that you receive from publishers and others who are judging the contest is well worth the nominal entry fee. And who knows, your game may even be taken home by an interested publisher!

## A Few Important Thoughts on Contests

Make sure to review the contest details and requirements closely. While some contests are open to any kind of game, some have restrictions as well.

Here are some of the restrictions you may see that you'll want to pay close attention to:

- Submission cannot be entered into any other contest
- Submission cannot have previously been available for sale or crowdfunded
- You must be able to attend the award ceremony
- You cannot publish the game submitted until the contest ends

If the contest is being hosted by a publisher, they might also indicate that the winner may be offered a contract to license your game (not guaranteed, though). Not a bad deal at all!

## Take Action

Check out the resources above to see if there are any upcoming contests. Check their requirements and timelines. If there's one that interests you, enter your game in the contest. What do you have to lose?

# 19

# Other Effective Approaches

> If you enjoy the whole process of creating games, then you'll keep creating them regardless of whether they get signed by a publisher. Then, it's only a matter of time before you'll have a game out in the world with your name on it.
>
> **– Emerson Matsuuchi**

Now, while I've already outlined the most common ways to get your game in front of a publisher, there are some other lesser-used techniques that you might want to consider.

## Using an Agent

If the thought of pitching your game to publishers makes you really nervous or bored out of your skull, or the cost and time needed to attend Conventions and meetups are too prohibitive, there is another alternative.

You could hire an agent to represent you and your game(s). In the toy world, these individuals are commonly referred to as "brokers."

This could be another experienced game designer whom you trust and who has a lot of connections. I have a friend who uses this approach and is happy to share the proceeds, as he understands that there is a lot of cost and time involved in attending these events, and he isn't interested in pitching his games himself. If the other designer is already going to these events and can set up meetings with publishers who may be interested in your game, this can be a very economical approach.

DOI: 10.1201/9781003334828-23

I've also pitched games for another designer with some success. The other designer was glad to have me do this for him, as he's not comfortable pitching his game to others and knew I was very familiar with his games and would do a good job for him.

Just remember that this other individual not only has to take the time to learn your game and be able to explain and teach it, but also has to be able to sell your game well. They may also be the one putting together your sell sheet and/or video and developing the pitch, depending on your arrangement. So, make sure they are compensated well for their time and efforts.

You could also choose to hire a professional agent to represent you. Make sure to do your homework if you go this route, making sure you hire somebody who will represent you professionally and have your best interests at heart. Get referrals and find an agent who has had success pitching games in the same genre as yours.

The fee for an agent may range from around 30% to 60% of your cut of any royalties, including advances. So, if you get a deal where you earn a 5% royalty on your game, you may end up with only 2–3% or so after the agent has taken his or her share. Still, 2–3% of something is better than 100% of nothing.

The benefit of using an agent is that you will save time and money upfront, allowing you to focus more on designing games than getting them signed. A good agent will likely have many contacts and may be able to get your game signed with the right publisher more easily. Of course, you have to pay for this benefit.

Here is a link (tinyurl.com/game-agents) to some potential "game and toy brokers."

## Go Online (Tabletop Simulator [TTS] or Tabletopia)

As I mentioned previously in Chapter 12, you can also create a digital version of your board game using tools like Tabletop Simulator and Tabletopia. These digital versions can be used to demo a game remotely with a publisher.

If you've already created a version of your game here, why not use it? Rather than travel to meet a publisher or only being able to share your game in pictures and words, demo your game to publishers online. You can talk to them in real time while you demo and answer any questions they have.

## Take Action

Determine your comfort level and ability to pitch to publishers, whether simply through emails or submission forms or by attending Cons and speed dating events. If you have no interest or capacity to do this all yourself, consider the alternative of hiring an agent, asking a friend or co-designer to pitch on your behalf in exchange for a percentage of the royalties and/or covering travel costs, or demoing the game online from the comfort of your home.

# Section IV

# What Publishers Want

# 20

# Questions Publishers Ask (and the Answers They Are Looking for)

Can I imagine myself teaching this at a convention booth, and having people actually stop and listen and want to play?

**– Paul Saxberg, Roxley Game Laboratory**

I've pitched my games to dozens of publishers and have been asked a lot of great questions about my games. In this chapter, I'll outline some of the most frequent questions I've been asked and what publishers are looking for, based on my experiences.

**Questions from publishers I've been asked or have heard**:

- How long have you been working on this game?
- Is this your first game?
- How many times have you playtested your game?
- What if we wanted to re-theme this as My Little Pony (or whatever)?
- Have you blind playtested your game?
- How does it play with different player counts?
- Have you tried this or that [insert various options/suggestions] in the game?
- What do people say about the game?
- How do experienced players and new players fare against each other?
- Have you run into any problems in the development? Are there any specific strategies most players take?

DOI: 10.1201/9781003334828-25

**My take on questions I've heard from publishers (responses to the above):**

When you meet with publishers, they will naturally have some questions for you about your game. The one thing you can do is be prepared.

I've met with dozens of publishers, many of whom have asked the same or similar questions. But in some cases, they also asked some very different questions.

It's always best to be honest. The following questions and responses will help you to determine if your game is ready for pitching, so that you can give honest answers that will have publishers knocking down your door to try your game.

## How Long Have You Been Working On This Game?

*Bad response:* Since yesterday.
*Another bad response:* Oh, about 10 years or so.
*Good response:* Six months to a year, with lots of playtesting, including some blind playtesting.

Publishers want to know that this isn't an idea you just came up with last night, but rather a game that has been playtested and iterated, and that it is fairly polished and at least nearing the state of completion. This means that the game plays very well consistently.

Also, if you say you've been working on this game for the last 10 or 15 years, this throws up a red flag. No game should take this long to develop, so many publishers might be wary of looking at a game such as this. Now, in fairness, you may not have been working on your game night and day, and it may have spent a lot of time on the shelf.

However, a publisher may think you are a little too meticulous as a designer or that you just have difficulty finishing something. They may also worry that you are too close to the project and will be unwilling to listen to suggestions on how to make the game better.

## Is This Your First Game?

*Bad response:* Yes, and it's going to be the next Monopoly!
*Another bad response:* No, this is my 700th game, but I don't have any published yet.

*Good response:* An honest one. If this is your first game, then say so. But if you're working on other games as well, don't be afraid to mention this.

It's ok if this is your first game. It's better to be honest about this upfront. If you have other games in the works, you can mention that this is one of many games you have in development, but that this is your first fully developed game or that none are published yet.

Publishers are likely to take you more seriously if you have a bit more experience. That's not to say that they won't consider a game which is your first, but you may stand a better chance if you have a few games under your belt (regardless of whether they have been published).

At the same time, if you've worked on a ton of games but haven't had a single one published, this may throw up a flag to publishers, who may perceive that you have difficulty finishing a project or may continuously bounce around between different ideas.

## How Many Times Have You Playtested Your Game? Who Have You Playtested This With?

*Bad response:* A few times with my Mom.
*Another bad response:* Playtesting? What's playtesting?
*Good response:* About 50 times with various groups, including other game designers.

While there is no magic number of playtests a game requires, publishers want to see that your game has been playtested a lot, especially by people you don't know directly who will give you honest, unbiased feedback.

It's fine to test out your game with friends and family at first, but after this, you have to put it in front of strangers and game designers as well, to see how they react to it. You also want to make sure it's been played and enjoyed by those who would be the ideal audience for your game.

A reasonably high number of playtests, usually at least 25, but often 50–100 or more may be necessary to work out most of the kinks and continuously iterate the game until it's at a phase where it plays well consistently. It just depends on the game. Some take more work, while others may come together quickly.

Quite often though, a publisher may not be interested in the exact number of playtests that you've done. They may be more interested in just seeing that your game is well-polished and plays really well and that it's not just an idea that you put together last night. They will often be able to see this for themselves. Every publisher is different. By playtesting your game a lot and making sure that it plays well, you'll stand a much better chance of having your game seriously considered.

## What If We Wanted to Re-Theme This as My Little Pony (or Whatever)?

*Bad response:* No way! My game is about raising corn and there's no way I'm changing it.
*Another bad response:* What's My Little Pony?
*Good response:* You're the expert. Whatever you feel would make the game the most successful.

With this question, publishers are really trying to get an idea of how easy it will be to work with you, more so than they want to paste a new theme on the game you've worked so hard to develop. While this particular question may be a bit extreme, your response will help publishers gauge whether you're going to be ok with them making business decisions related to your game or if you're going to fight them every step of the way.

Generally, when a publisher picks up your game, they can do whatever they want with it. This includes renaming, re-theming, or making any other changes they see fit. They have presumably been in the industry for many years and know what sells and what doesn't. Publishing and marketing a game are very different from creating one. Sometimes you just have to let it go and allow other professionals to do what they do best.

## Have You Blind Playtested This Game?

*Bad response:* No.
*Another bad response:* Blind playtesting? You mean, like with someone visually impaired?
*Good response:* Yes, I've blind playtested this with a few different groups, and they seemed to grasp all the rules and gameplay very well. I've updated the rules based on my observations and it plays really smoothly without my intervention.

Blind playtesting is a crucial step in the design process. While it's not critical that you have done blind playtesting before pitching your game to a publisher, it certainly can be very beneficial. It shows that you have tested the game with people who have never seen it before, to ensure that the rules and gameplay all make sense. When somebody later buys your game, they won't have you there in their living room to explain what happens when you draw the attack card, so you'd better make sure that your rules are solid, either before pitching or as you develop the game with the publisher.

## How Does It Play With Different Player Counts?

*Bad response:* I've only playtested it as a two-player game (but the game is meant for two to six players).
*Another bad response:* Pretty well I'm sure.
*Good response:* I've playtested this multiple times at each player count, and it plays really well at all of them.

If you claim that your game is meant for three to eight players, you want to be confident that it plays well at each of these player counts. Now, there may be a sweet spot where the game is that much better, say when you have five or more players, which you can highlight for the publisher.

Some games play very differently when you change the number of players. At a lower player count, there may be a lot less interaction (or it may become a "take that" style of game), whereas at a higher player count the game may become too restrictive, or players may get bored waiting for their turn. It's not to say that the game will be exactly the same experience with three players compared to a full game with eight players, however, it should play well at every player count that you have identified.

## Have You Tried This or That [Insert Various Options/Suggestions] in the Game?

*Bad response:* I don't like games like that.
*Another bad response:* No way, that's a terrible idea!
*Good response:* Actually, I haven't, but that's an interesting idea. I'll have to try that out to see how it works and if it makes the game even better.

When a publisher first looks at or plays your game, they may have some ideas about how to potentially improve upon it. While not every thought will be gold, remember that they do have a lot of experience, and it is worth considering these ideas.

Their suggestion may actually be something you have tried already. If this is the case, you can let them know that this is a great idea, and you had implemented it previously, and then explain what happened and why it is no longer part of the game.

Remember, publishers are not only interested in your game, but also working with you as a person. You want to be receptive to their questions and suggestions. Thank them for their ideas, and if you have the opportunity, try them out and see if they improve your game further.

## What Do People Say About the Game?

*Bad response:* This is going to be the next Monopoly!
*Another bad response:* Well, my mom loves it!
*Good response:* Most people love the strategy and tough decisions they have to make, and some even ask if they can buy a copy or when it will be available.

As always, honesty is the best policy. If people are saying this is going to be the next Monopoly, then that shows the publisher that the people you've been playing with don't necessarily know modern board games. If your mom loves it, great. But your mom probably loves everything you do, or at least says so.

Again, you'll want to have playtested your game with a variety of people, including total strangers who are willing to give honest and unbiased feedback. Take note of what they're saying, fixing problems that are identified along the way, and let the publisher know exactly what these players like about your game.

If everyone who plays your game asks if they can play again, that's a great sign, and something you'll want to share with the publisher. If they want to buy your game right on the spot, don't be afraid to toot your own horn and let the publisher know.

## How Do Experienced Players and New Players Fare against Each Other?

*Bad response:* The new player almost always wins.
*Another bad response:* I've only played this with the same group, so they're all equally experienced.
*Good response:* The new player will often be beaten by the experienced player the first time, but immediately asks for a rematch. The second match is usually much closer, but the experienced player tends to win more often.

I should preface that the responses above are more suited to a game with some level of strategy, as opposed to a family or children's game which may rely heavily on luck. In the case of a more luck-driven game, you may be trying to level the playing field between kids and adults, or experienced and inexperienced players, which could be completely appropriate for this type of game.

But for a more strategic game, a publisher may be concerned about new players being "blown out of the water" so to speak, by an experienced player, leading the new player to never want to play the game again. Hopefully, if your game is interesting enough, the new player may just be getting a feel for the game the first time they play, and then start to think about different strategies they may take the next time they play. This could lead to a closer result the next time, or perhaps the new player taking the victory.

Depending on the game, publishers may be interested in seeing the experienced player having a distinct advantage. In the case of chess, an experienced player will almost always demolish an inexperienced one. This may or may not be what the publisher is looking for in their own line of games, but it will be good for them to know how experience level changes the feel of the game.

Watch out for first or last player advantages in your game as well. Make sure to always keep track of scores at the end of playtests, ordering the player's names from first to last player, to see if there is any trend. If you see a positional advantage, you will want to do something in the design to even the playing field well before approaching a publisher.

## Have You Run into Any Problems in the Development? Are There Any Specific Strategies Most Players Take?

*Bad response:* No, the game plays perfectly.
*Another bad response:* Yeah, everyone seems to hate all the tedious manual scoring at the end, but I love that part!
*Good response:* At one point, I found that all players were making the same choice at a particular part of the game, so I introduced some new interesting choices, which resulted in a lot more varied gameplay.

I'll say it again: be honest. If there were any major flaws, you can mention them, along with what you did to fix the issue. This shows the publisher that you are capable of identifying problems and finding viable solutions.

It doesn't matter so much what *you* think of the game, rather it has to do with how players perceive the gameplay. Just because you like a certain aspect of the game, that doesn't mean this will make the final cut, especially if players dislike this part.

Perhaps players tend to play a certain way the first time. As they play it more, they may develop interesting strategies or take different paths. It will be good for the publisher to know this, so they know what to expect if they take a prototype with them and run their own playtests.

## Take Action

Prepare yourself for all of the questions in this chapter before meeting with any publishers in person. This will help you to build your confidence and increase your chances of success in having that publisher walk away from your meeting wanting to work with you and move forward with your game.

# 21

# Advice from Real Publishers

> I consider if any of my brands have a built-in audience. Then I consider if the game has the potential to stand out in the market.
>
> **– Joshua Lobkowicz, Grey Fox Games**

I reached out to several publishers with some common questions that designers have, and many were kind enough to answer these questions and provide some other really helpful information.

I've outlined each of the questions that I asked these publishers and have summarized the key findings from these responses in this chapter. Each publisher's exact response to these specific questions can be found in the following chapter as well.

In some cases, a publisher shared an article or other helpful information, which has been included at the end of this chapter, with their permission.

**What are the key things you're looking for when you hear a pitch from a designer (in a sell sheet, in a video, and in-person)?**

Be concise with each of these.

*Sell sheet*—Concise component counts, demographics (age, number of players, play time), what is fun and unique about the game, the hook, the mechanics.

*Video*—Similar to the sell sheet, keep it under 5 minutes, show actual gameplay, high-level overview, and hook, not a full rules explanation.

*In-person*—All of the above, keep very brief for a pitch (if it's a longer meeting, let them play at least a turn or two), show your excitement or passion for the game, and if you're not good at this, either work on your pitching skills or have someone else present the game on your behalf.

DOI: 10.1201/9781003334828-26

**What level of prototype would you expect from a designer (in terms of look, art, and polish)?**

Your game should be mechanically sound and understandable. Placeholder art is fine to express the theme and feeling. Finalized art can sometimes be a red flag (inexperienced designer). Changes must be expected, so a designer can't be too invested in this.

**Can you walk us through the thought processes as you're looking at a game?**

Is it fun and interesting? Am I having a good time while playing? How could I make this game into a product? What changes would make it even better? What is the hook or what makes this game stand out? What kind of table presence does the game have? Does it fit one of our existing brands or our catalog? Could expansions be made?

**What are the top three questions that you like to ask a designer when discussing a game of theirs that you might be interested in, and what types of responses are you looking for with each of them?**

1. **How much has the game been tested/how long have you been working on it?**
   Publishers want to know that your game has been well tested and is far along in the process.
2. **How would you feel about [change or suggestions for the game]?**
   Publishers want to gauge how it will be to work with you as a designer. Are you open to changes? Are you going to be easy to work with?
3. **Why did you create this game and what makes it different and more fun than other games?**
   Publishers want to know what inspired your game and how it will sell. Can they make it into a product that people will love and want to buy?

**What are the factors that make you most likely to sign a game from a designer?**

Both the game and the game designer have to be a good fit for the publisher. Also, the game should be amazing!

**Let's say a designer has given you their prototype for a game you are interested in. How long should they wait to follow up with you if they**

**haven't heard back and what's the best approach they can take to not come across as pushy or demanding?**

A publisher should be able to give you a rough timeline for when you can expect to hear back from them. If this time passes, you should feel free to contact them, or if this was not specified, it is usually good to reach out to the publisher after about a month. As long as you approach the publisher professionally and respectfully, a little reminder is often seen as helpful, not pushy.

**How long is your typical production time from contract signing to game release?**

This depends greatly on how much more development work is needed, as well as by the publisher and method of distribution (Kickstarter, retail, distributors, etc.). This is often at least a year but could range anywhere from 6 months to 3 years.

**How involved do you want a designer to be in the production of the game once the contract has been signed and you have it in your possession? What responsibilities are yours, and which ones are the designer's?**

Most publishers want a designer to be as involved or as hands-off as the designer chooses. The designer does have to keep in mind, however, that while the publisher may ask for a designer's opinion, the publisher has the final say.

**What is the typical type and frequency of communication you have with the designer between signing the contract and releasing the game?**

This depends on the game and the involvement of the designer. Communication is often via email and is usually more frequent during the development process.

**If you pass on a game, what is your policy or approach about returning a prototype?**

Most publishers are very willing to send back a prototype to a designer. Some will only do so at a designer's expense, so it is best to check with the publisher if or when this occurs.

**What types of games are you looking for? What would excite you to see come across your desk?**

Naturally, the responses to this question varied from publisher to publisher. The exact responses from each publisher are detailed in the next chapter.

**How do you prefer to be contacted or meet (email, setting up a meeting at a convention, speed dating event, other?) and what would you like to see when you are contacted (sell sheet, overview video, rules, live demo)?**

Many publishers preferred meeting face-to-face, however, please see the next chapter for the details provided by each publisher.

**What is the best way to contact you (please provide email/form link/alternate contact information)?**

The responses to this question are provided in the next chapter for each publisher.

## Other Helpful Advice from Publishers (Reprinted With Permission)

*Stonemaier Games*

Submission Guidelines (https://stonemaiergames.com/about/submission-guidelines/)

**We are currently closed for submissions.** However, you may still submit your game to us, and when we reopen submissions (possibly in mid/late 2020), we will review the form below.

HOW TO SUBMIT: *Please fill out this form.* That's it!

IF WE LIKE YOUR PITCH: We'll contact you and arrange to see the game in more detail through ONE of the following (usually your choice):

Pre-recorded video of you and your friends playing the game A prototype sent to us

In-person at a convention

As a participant of our annual *Design Day.* We don't actually hear pitches at Design Day, but we look at all the games other designers bring to it.

You can read more about the various steps in our submission process *here.*

*Guidelines and Requirements*

Carefully read our *12 Tenets of Game Design*. Watching *this video* may help too.

We're looking for tabletop games (not RPGs) that *capture our imaginations.*

The player count must accommodate a minimum of 2 players (we'll probably add a solo variant to take it down to 1) and an upper range of at least 5, 6, or greater. We'll ignore submissions for 2–4 player games.

We're looking for *event* games–the featured main course at game night, not the appetizer or side salad–that play in 1–2 hours.

We're looking for *unique* games—your game must feature something that has not been done before.

A player's turn should be short and simple, and players should dictate the flow of play, not the game. If your game has a number of phases (either within each player's turn or within each round), please don't submit it to us.

### *Your Game Must Be*

**Fully Created, Not Just an Idea:** *Ideas are important but largely worthless.* Actually taking a game from a concept to a fully-formed creation is a completely different matter–that's what we're looking for.

**Polished and Playtested:** Part of our role as the publisher is to playtest and arrange for blind playtesting of your game beyond the scope of what you can do. But it's still your responsibility to extensively playtest (and blind playtest) your game before sending it to us.

**Playable**: The #1 mistake we see is that the prototypes we receive are unplayable, either due to the rules, the lack of reference cards, or other factors that could have been solved by blind playtesting. You get one chance to make a first impression, and if that involves an unplayable game, we're not going to publish it.

**Thoughtfully Graphic Designed:** It's our responsibility to make the game look great in terms of art and graphic design. However, submitting your game to us without any art or thoughtful design will make the playtesting process very difficult. Please use placeholder art that reflects how you view the world of your game and be intentional with your graphic design for the final prototype—user interface matters. Do not commission final art, though—that's our responsibility as a publisher.

**Rules:** We need to be able to figure out how to play the game by reading the rules. Just as with any written work, confusing writing, poor English, and numerous typos will negatively affect our impression of your work. A Microsoft Word file is completely fine, but please try to insert examples and photographs/images throughout the rules.

**Flexibility:** We may love your game, but there's still a high chance that we'll have some changes we want to make it better and more marketable. Please be clear with us upfront if there are certain changes you will never consider. If you won't consider any changes, you're not a good fit for us.

**Unique:** We're looking for unique themes and mechanisms—please, no pirates, zombies, Cthulhu, or trains. Jamey typically does not enjoy stock games, tactical combat games (or games that primarily focus on combat/war), hidden-movement games, party games, take-that games, punishing games, programming, and dungeon crawlers but *there are exceptions to those preferences.*

**Hooks**: Your game should have one or more *hooks.*

### *Why Would You Want Us to Publish Your Game?*

**We'll be honest with you.** If you're deciding between publishing the game yourself via Kickstarter or submitting it to publishers like Stonemaier, please consider the pros and cons of each. If you self-publish, you can build a business, you have full creative control, and you'll make more money if the game is successful but *it will involve a lot more work.* If you just want to design games, submitting them to a publisher may be a better fit for you.

**We're focused.** We don't publish many games, which means that when we release a game, we make a big deal about it and support it for a long time.

**We're passionate.** We're not trying to pump out games that we barely know or care about. Rather, we focus a ton of time, energy, and money on games we truly love, the games that we're happy to share with the world as if they are our own. If you want that type of passion and drive at the helm of your game, you're at the right place.

**We love games.** We truly love tabletop games. Hopefully, you will find that to be the case for any publisher, but it's worth mentioning that our love of games is why we do this. We're not in it for the money—we're here to connect thousands of people with memorable, fun gaming experiences. If that's what drives you too, we can build amazing things together.

**We're a partner, not an employer.** We want to make the best version of your game. That means collaborating with you to make sure we stay true to your vision while enhancing and elevating various aspects of the game. We will ask for your opinions, thoughts, and permission throughout the process.

## Nick Bentley at North Star Games

(https://www.nickbentley.games/bad-board-game-design-pitches/)

I work for *North Star Games*, where one of my jobs is to listen to pitches from game designers who want to license their games.

I see more than a hundred pitches a year and I'm astounded by how bad they are. 99% are bad. No exaggeration.

**Here's the problem:**

More than 4,000 board games are published annually. Thanks to all that competition, fantastic gameplay is just table stakes. A game also has to be a great *product*, which means it must satisfy some constraints *in addition to* fantastic gameplay. Most designers, especially hobby game designers, don't address the product side in their pitches or do it poorly.

I can boil the product side of a pitch down to two key questions:

**Question #1: What is UNIQUELY awesome about this game?**

I mean UNIQUE. I want to know what it has *that no other game has*. The answer could relate to the theme, mechanism, feel, components, potential art, etc. When I ask designers this question, they usually answer in one of two ways:

1. **They point to a not-unique feature,** for example: "It's a really social game and plays great with 7 players", or "There's a ton of tension in the bidding". But those descriptions apply to other games and they don't sell copies.
2. **They point to a unique but banal feature**, usually some small twist on gameplay that isn't enough of a head-turner. For example: "It's a route-making game along the lines of Ticket to Ride but you have to buy easements to make your routes."—the kind of thing you'd expect to find in an expansion or variant of a preexisting game brand. It doesn't matter if it's awesome to you, the designer. All that matters is whether it's awesome to the people who would buy the game.

With additional prodding, it usually becomes clear the game has no feature which is both actually unique and actually awesome. We can't bring a game like that into the current market and expect it to have *any* chance of being a hit. That means we can't publish it because this is a hit-driven industry: staying in business depends on hits. So, it's essential for us to see a potential path to Hitsville for each game we publish. That brings us to the second question:

**Question #2: How will this game become a hit?**

For a game to be a hit, it not only has to be uniquely awesome, but it also has to find its audience. How will it do that?

If you can tell a story about how the publisher can reach the game's audience, you have a huge leg up. Ideally, the game is perfectly tailored to the audience the publisher already has. For example, my company is best known among hobby gamers for our *Evolution-themed games*. As a result, many of our fans have a scientific worldview and love nature. If you have a uniquely awesome way to embody those values in a game, it's easy for us to show it to people who care.

But there are other ways too. Maybe you're friends with Beyonce and she's agreed to share it on Instagram. Maybe you have convincing data that an unusually high number of people who play the game evangelize it to their friends. Maybe you already made an app of it and it has 10,000 active players. Maybe you've discovered an audience during your market research that other publishers don't yet know exists, so there's low competition. The only limit is your creativity.

**Answer the above questions first**

Until I've got good answers to the above questions, I don't want to know details about your game. So, address these product issues at the top of your pitch. Be succinct, specific, and concrete. No superlatives and minimize adjectives. The template for your pitch is:

1. "This is a [what kind of game is it] game where you [what players do in the game]"
2. "The uniquely awesome thing about it is [uniquely awesome thing]"
3. "Here's how the game will be a hit"

If you knock these arguments out of the park, I can figure everything else out for myself via follow-up questions and playtesting (tip: don't talk about how good the gameplay is. That's what playtesting is for).

**This isn't rocket science. Why do so few game designers do this? Two reasons:**

They don't fully appreciate how severe the competition has become and what games must be to succeed now.

They design games for themselves, and then only think about how to turn them into products after they're finished.

**A deeper problem**

The second point above is instructive because it means the problem runs deeper than pitching. The problem is the design process.

To make a publishable game, write down a game's pitch BEFORE you start designing it. Try to come up with a concept that's a *significant* departure from what already exists in some key way that will matter to people, and which isn't too hard to communicate. A classic example is the idea of a legacy game: "A game where the rules change each time you play, depending on what happens in each game". That's the kind of thing you should be shooting for.

**After you've come up with your concept:**

- Get feedback from gamer friends about whether they think it's a cool idea. Pro tip: show them pitches for a few different concepts and ask them to pick their favorite. Giving them a basis for comparison makes it *way* easier to interpret their responses.
- If you decide the pitch is good enough to make a publishable game of it, let it be your guide for the design. Ask yourself over and over: "How can I refine this game to better satisfy the promise of the pitch?'
- Use the evolving game design to explore how to improve the pitch further, so the pitch and the design evolve *together*.

Finally, if you're pitching your game in-person, *practice your pitch* until every word of every sentence is perfect, and it comes out right every time.

**A proposition for game designers**

I've got a mutually beneficial proposal for you game designers. I'll be more successful if I can find designers who heed the advice above, and you'll be more successful if you heed it. So, I've provided a worksheet below, where you can write down and refine your pitches for games over time, as you work on them.

I've made it a Google survey so I can see who's using it and how. If I see you putting together a great pitch, I'll get in touch with you. Maybe I can help. I won't use or share anything input here without your permission.

(form embedded on-page – link at the start of this article)

# 22

# Publisher-Specific Wants and Needs

> A prototype doesn't have to be polished; it just needs to be able to clearly convey the core game mechanisms. The fun should shine through the rough materials.
>
> **– Jason Schneider, Gamewright**

In this chapter, I've shared the exact responses I received from each of the publishers that responded to the survey. They appear in the order they were received.

Please note that this information is accurate at the time of publication, however, publishers may change what they are looking for in a game over time. Always check a publisher's website to see if they are currently accepting submissions and what they are looking for before pitching them your game.

## Publisher

Gold Nugget Games

## Name

Cody Thompson

**What are the key things you're looking for when you hear a pitch from a designer (in a sell sheet, in a video, and in-person)?**

*Sell Sheet*—Game stats (player count, time, etc.), concise component lists (108 poker-sized cards, NOT 10 player cards, 50 item cards, etc.), and a

DOI: 10.1201/9781003334828-27

concise hook to the game, no wall of text. You have 5–10 seconds max of me looking at a sell sheet to hook me.

*Video*—Short and sweet, ideally under 5 minutes, 2–3 preferably. Super high-level overview of the game, not every rule of the game and instance where it happens. Excitement and hook, why would I want to play this game.

*In-person*—Excitement about the game. If you aren't excited about it, why should I be? Concise pitch. I don't want a 30-minute rules explanation. Put pieces in my hand and tell me what to do. I would much rather spend 10 minutes on the game and 20 minutes on you, the person. If I sign the game, I will spend a LOT of time with it. You, I may only ever meet that one time.

**What level of prototype would you expect from a designer (in terms of look, art, and polish)?**

I expect it to be mechanically complete as far as you can take it. A feeling of the theme and the art can help a lot. Don't get the whole game illustrated, but maybe get one to two pieces done to evoke the feeling that you intend. Most importantly, just have a functional graphic design. I want to be able to playtest the game quickly, not spend the whole time trying to figure out what a card does.

**Can you walk us through the thought processes as you're looking at a game?**

The first thing I look at is the theme, and if it's something I'm interested in, then I look at the components and envision how I would make this a cool product. Then I make sure that there is a fun experience to the game and that the mechanics aren't getting in the way of the fun.

**What are the top three questions that you like to ask a designer when discussing a game of theirs you might be interested in, and what types of responses are you looking for with each of them?**

1. **Who you are**
   I want to know you as a person.
2. **Why should I sign this game?**
   Looking for what's special about the game, AND why I, in particular, should publish it. Gloomhaven is great, but I am not publishing that anytime soon. Also, if it's special, but not for me, I may be able to give suggestions to pitch to other publishers that it better aligns with.

3. **One piece of critical feedback**
   This is an important part as I want to see how designers respond to feedback. If I sign the game, I am going to tear apart every aspect of the game to validate if it is needed. There will most likely be lots of changes, big or small. A designer must be able to stomach that process.

**What are the factors that make you most likely to sign a game from a designer?**

The theme, if it's in the style of game I am looking for, and the designer.

**Let's say a designer has given you their prototype for a game you are interested in. How long should they wait to follow up with you if they haven't heard back and what's the best approach they can take to not come across as pushy or demanding?**

I may be in the rarity, but I welcome emails at any time with any questions. Typically, I would say check in every 1–3 months.

**How long is your typical production time from contract signing to game release?**

Currently about 3 years, but I am a one-person company. I'm looking to get it down to one and a half to two years.

**How involved do you want a designer to be in the production of the game once the contract has been signed and you have it in your possession? What responsibilities are yours, and which ones are the designer's?**

I want the designer to be as involved or hands-off as they would personally like. Just set the expectation upfront.

**What is the typical type and frequency of communication you have with the designer between signing the contract and releasing the game?**

Early in the process probably once per month. Middle, probably once every 3 months. Late in the process, once or more per month. But I am looking to increase this amount of communication, as well as develop a way for all of the designers and myself to have casual conversations.

**If you pass on a game, what is your policy or approach about returning a prototype?**

Whatever the designer would like. I would appreciate money for shipping it, but I typically just pay for it myself since I feel bad for rejecting the game.

**What types of games are you looking for? What would excite you to see come across your desk?**

Easy to learn, unique but familiar theme, streamlined gameplay.

**How do you prefer to be contacted or meet (email, setting up a meeting at a convention, speed dating event, other?) and what would you like to see when you are contacted (sell sheet, overview video, rules, live demo)?**

In-person is the best but least likely. The second would be my submission form on my website and/or email. I want as much information as you have—sell sheet, video, playtester feedback. All of it. I don't want to have to continue emailing for more information.

**What is the best way to contact you (please provide email/form link/alternate contact information)?**

cody@goldnuggetgames.com

## Publisher

Roxley Game Laboratory

## Name

Paul Saxberg

**What are the key things you're looking for when you hear a pitch from a designer (in a sell sheet, in a video, and in-person)?**

Brevity and clarity for all three. If you can't figure out how to summarize your game in three sentences, find a friend or fellow designer who can. Please don't spend a lot of time telling us your game is awesome. We already know you think your game is awesome.

*Sell sheet:* Mechanics, length, and the number of players, components.

*Video:* PLEASE make your video 5 minutes or less and please demonstrate one to two or more actual turns of gameplay. Professional production is NOT necessary, but if I can't conceptualize how to play your game after watching it for 5 minutes, I am likely going to think it's too complicated for our customers to understand and for me to teach (I also have too many other messages to answer, so I am going to send you a form letter and skip ahead to the next designer who did make their video five minutes).

*In-person:* All of the above applies, but unfortunately, the best thing you can do to improve your in-person pitch is to work on your interpersonal skills rather than your game. If this terrifies you, convince a friend who is a better pitch person than you to help you demo. I've had teams pitch me games before.

**What level of prototype would you expect from a designer (in terms of look, art, and polish)?**

Functionality is the primary concern. Beyond that, I would create just enough atmosphere using clipart, temporary art, etc. to try to create the aesthetic you would prefer to see in the game. If you have clearly invested a lot of money into original artwork and a professional prototype, that is actually a potential red flag against you and your game, as it means there's a high chance you are inexperienced in the industry, and/or that you don't listen to feedback, and/or that you will be less open to changes or a retheme.

**Can you walk us through the thought processes as you're looking at a game?**

1. Can I imagine myself teaching this at a convention booth, and having people actually stop and listen and want to play?
2. Almost always, I start imagining what I would add or change or suggest or would like to try.
3. I'm watching the designer to see how they react to questions, critiques, suggestions, commentary. Defensiveness is not a great sign but it's not necessarily a dealbreaker (especially if the designer's answers indicate a thorough understanding of the problem. Example: "Yes, that problem did come up sometimes in testing; but after adjusting costs on the X cards and changing the turn order mechanic, it was only a problem on the last turn, and by then players are already focused on something else").

**What are the top three questions that you like to ask a designer when discussing a game of theirs you might be interested in, and what types of responses are you looking for with each of them?**

1. **How much has this been tested?**
   Answer: LOTS, with a wide variety of people, and it's been changed a lot based on all that testing.

2. **How open are you to major changes, developments, suggestions, retheme?**
   Answer: An open mind. That is not the same as, "I'll just auto-agree to anything you say", but someone that will intelligently discuss things that are raised, understanding that we have our own expertise and experience we bring to the table (or you wouldn't be talking to us in the first place).
3. **Are you flexible about "maybe", unknown timelines, exclusivity, etc.?**
   We do not wish to be unfair to anyone and prefer to get these questions addressed early, but our schedule is very much subject to change.

**What are the factors that make you most likely to sign a game from a designer?**

1. Game is freaking amazing and fun to play. People want to play it again immediately after playing it once. Literally, nothing trumps this factor.
2. We can see a way for us to make it into a marketable product, preferably on Kickstarter.
3. Unusual or innovative design, mechanics, or approach.
4. We can't see ways to improve or change it. It is publishable as is. So far, we have yet to run into this game, but we hold out hope.

**Let's say a designer has given you their prototype for a game you are interested in. How long should they wait to follow up with you if they haven't heard back and what's the best approach they can take to not come across as pushy or demanding?**

Checking in is NOT pushy or demanding if it is done politely and professionally. In fact, it can be a very good thing. I would suggest asking for a good timeline to check in at when you actually send in the game, or if you forgot that step, one to two months, or if the publisher is late messaging you, one to two weeks after they should have.

**How long is your typical production time from contract signing to game release?**

Highly variable in our case. We want it to be faster but currently are not able to make guarantees.

**How involved do you want a designer to be in the production of the game once the contract has been signed and you have it in your**

**possession? What responsibilities are yours, and which ones are the designer's?**

This answer depends very much on the game and the designer. In a perfect world, the designer is no longer needed once the game is signed, but we do not live in a perfect world, so, ideally, we want the designer on board for intelligent discussion of the evolutions of the game. We like to consult the designer on product design and art, but we normally need to be in charge of those. We welcome the designer's assistance in promoting the game on social media, BGG, Kickstarter comments, conventions that are easy to go to, etc.

**What is the typical type and frequency of communication you have with the designer between signing the contract and releasing the game?**

Ideally, we hope a designer has Discord and can be in regular contact with us there. It depends on the game and the designer.

**If you pass on a game, what is your policy or approach about returning a prototype?**

We are prepared to return a prototype to a designer on request.

**What types of games are you looking for? What would excite you to see come across your desk?**

Type or theme of the game almost doesn't matter what excites me is when I look at the dozen or so cold-call submissions in my inbox that week and I find one that I actually want to sit down and play.

Innovation is one way to capture this kind of attention. A quick summary that gives us an idea of what gameplay experience we should imagine ourselves getting in for is a good thing.

**How do you prefer to be contacted or meet (email, setting up a meeting at a convention, speed dating event, other?) and what would you like to see when you are contacted (sell sheet, overview video, rules, live demo)?**

Email cold calls honestly have a low chance of succeeding but are probably still your best chance. Ideally, you should include a paragraph describing the game, a video of 5 minutes or less in which you actually show some gameplay and how to play, and your rulebook. Big bonus points if your game is on Tabletop Simulator and can be easily evaluated there.

We have had very poor results with speed dating, unfortunately, and will not likely pursue it in the future.

We won't be attending many conventions in the near future, and we generally don't schedule meetings with designers at conventions unless we are already interested because of the previous contact. You can certainly cold call us in person. We will not be offended by this, but be aware it will be a long shot.

**What is the best way to contact you (please provide email/form link/ alternate contact information)?**

info@roxley.com

# Publisher

XYZ Game Labs

# Name

Adam McCrimmon

**What are the key things you're looking for when you hear a pitch from a designer (in a sell sheet, in a video, and in-person)?**

- Type of game (bluffing, worker placement, hidden role, party, roll/ write, euro, tile placement, etc)
- Length per player and number of players (Bonus: Best at players)
- Theme (Bonus: Why did you choose this theme?)
- Hook - What makes this special?
- Win Condition(s)
- Game play overview

**What level of prototype would you expect from a designer (in terms of look, art, and polish)?**

It doesn't matter. In fact, the more "polished" it is the less likely we are to take a hard look at it unless the designer is really upfront about being ok with any theme changes.

**Can you walk us through the thought processes as you're looking at a game?**

The first look is really a test of whether or not this hooks us as being interesting. Maybe it's a unique theme, mechanic, or gameplay. Maybe it's the type of game and length that intrigues us. At its core, every game we publish will eventually need to be a consumer product. Consumer products have a hook that makes people interested in buying them. So, the first test is: Is there a hook? There are just too many designs out there for us to spend time on something that DOESN'T have a hook.

The second step is for us to play the game because before we do anything else, we obviously want to know if this is a good, fun, and interesting game.

The third step is to figure out what we think is missing or needs to be changed to make it both gameplay and product viable. If that list is too big or onerous—we'll give notes to the designer and pass on it for now. If not: then we discuss what we thought and how we might want to change/update the design or theme. If the designer agrees, then we'll move forward.

The fourth step is design/theme/development. We like the designers of the games we publish to be involved in the process. So, to ensure this works well for both of us we invest some time in the project from a design, theme, and development standpoint. This usually lasts a month or two. In the end, we make a final call based on the results of that work and the relationship with the designer.

**What are the top three questions that you like to ask a designer when discussing a game of theirs you might be interested in, and what types of responses are you looking for with each of them?**

1. Why did you make this?
2. What is your favorite part?
3. What is the weakest part of this design?

In general, I am looking for honest, open, and transparent answers. The substance is less important than how the questions are answered. If we're going to work with someone going forward, we have to know that we can have honest two-way communication.

**What are the factors that make you most likely to sign a game from a designer?**

Good game. Great working relationship. Great company catalog fit.

**Let's say a designer has given you their prototype for a game you are interested in. How long should they wait to follow up with you if they**

**haven't heard back and what's the best approach they can take to not come across as pushy or demanding?**

Give us a month to check it out and then just send over an email asking for an update. Ideally, we get to all submissions within 30 days. But in the case where we don't, it's because we're spread thin during that time.

Hitting us up at the 30-day mark will ensure that we bump it up in priority.

**How long is your typical production time from contract signing to game release?**

We have a rough plan that goes out 2–3 years. There are always places where things can move or projects that might have a good reason to break into that timeline. It all depends on the project and game. At the low end, it's 9–12 months. On the high side, it's 24–36 months.

**How involved do you want a designer to be in the production of the game once the contract has been signed and you have it in your possession? What responsibilities are yours, and which ones are the designer's?**

From our point of view, we're responsible for everything once it's signed. However, we want our designers to be involved and have an opinion about how it's being presented, the art, the development—pretty much everything because their name will be on this. However, it's important to note: Once we own the rights, we're going to make the call that makes the most sense for us. Every suggestion and opinion from the designer will be considered and debated, but not necessarily implemented.

**What is the typical type and frequency of communication you have with the designer between signing the contract and releasing the game?**

That is really dependent on the project timeline, type of game, release plans, etc.

**If you pass on a game, what is your policy or approach about returning a prototype?**

Default: we'll send it back to you.

**What types of games are you looking for? What would excite you to see come across your desk?**

My current wishlist as of November 2019:

- A social deduction game for 2–6+ players

- A rich/heavy game that plays in an hour or less
- Anything that fits our "Quarks" line (pocket games that you can learn and play in under 30 minutes)
- An elegant abstract that works as both a gateway game and a more in-depth experience

**How do you prefer to be contacted or meet (email, setting up a meeting at a convention, speed dating event, other?) and what would you like to see when you are contacted (sell sheet, overview video, rules, live demo)?**

Meetings at cons are impossible to ignore, so those are GREAT. But even just reaching out on Twitter or email works. The best thing to send me: An under 3-minute video explaining the game. Nothing helps me make a go or no-go decision faster than seeing a game in action.

**What is the best way to contact you (please provide email/form link/alternate contact information)?**

adam@xyzgamelabs.com or @McAtoms on Twitter.

## Publisher

KTBG/Burnt Island Games

## Name

Helaina Cappel

**What are the key things you're looking for when you hear a pitch from a designer (in a sell sheet, in a video, and in-person)?**

Who is the game for, how is it different than other games, and how much fun will players have.

**What level of prototype would you expect from a designer (in terms of look, art, and polish)?**

Prototypes don't have to have art, but the designer should have thought about what components the game will need to have in its final form. There should be some sense of design in the mechanisms and aesthetics.

**Can you walk us through the thought processes as you're looking at a game?**

The first thing I look for is table presence. If it doesn't immediately catch my eye, it probably isn't for us. Once I know that there is something special about the game, I'll look at what the game has to offer to players. I'm looking for games for two brands, so it's pretty broad for me. At the same time, it's very specific. KTBG is always looking for games that are for adults but that kids can play. So, I am looking for something in the game that can level the playing field, whether it be in catch-up mechanisms or the approachability of the game. For Burnt Island, I am looking for innovation. I want to make games that have familiar mechanisms but turn them on their side so that they seem new and fresh. Once I have established these few things, I know we have a game that is worth developing.

**What are the top three questions that you like to ask a designer when discussing a game of theirs you might be interested in, and what types of responses are you looking for with each of them?**

1. How many times have you tested this game?
2. How many times did you test this game with kids?
3. What was the reaction of the kids when they played the game?

My expected response is always that they have played the game many, many times with both kids and adults. I also expect that they tell me the reaction they got from both kids and adults, not just that they liked the game. Tell me about what they were doing when they played. Tell me about what they were saying to each other when they played. Tell me if they kept talking about the game after they left the table.

**What are the factors that make you most likely to sign a game from a designer?**

I need to know that a designer is not finished designing when they start working with us. Very rarely does a publisher get a game in their hands that doesn't need development. When a designer can work with the publisher to develop their game, that's a pretty important piece of the puzzle.

**Let's say a designer has given you their prototype for a game you are interested in. How long should they wait to follow up with you if they**

**haven't heard back and what's the best approach they can take to not come across as pushy or demanding?**

I always feel it best to tell a designer right away if we are interested in their game. If we are interested and want a prototype, we'll keep it for a while. If it gets to the table right away, it means that we loved it from the outset, and will typically be signed very soon after we get it. If we're waiting on getting it to the table, we aren't that excited about it. A designer should give it a couple of weeks before a follow-up.

**How long is your typical production time from contract signing to game release?**

We try to make the timeline no longer than 2 years from the first play to being on store shelves. Often it takes 8–10 months to get it to Kickstarter, and another 8–10 months to get it onto shelves.

**How involved do you want a designer to be in the production of the game once the contract has been signed and you have it in your possession? What responsibilities are yours, and which ones are the designer's?**

I expect the designer to weigh in on each process from development to art. Once the game is produced though, the rest is up to us. Marketing and sales are our expertise, so the designer should never have to feel like they need to have those skills also.

**What is the typical type and frequency of communication you have with the designer between signing the contract and releasing the game?**

The most communication happens within the time we are developing the game. Typically, there is a lot of communication during the Kickstarter portion as well.

**If you pass on a game, what is your policy or approach about returning a prototype?**

I respectfully decline it through an email and send it back to the designer.

**What types of games are you looking for? What would excite you to see come across your desk?**

I think the previous questions covered this. Games that are either new and fresh with great table presence, or games that have tried and true mechanisms, but innovatively use them.

**How do you prefer to be contacted or meet (email, setting up a meeting at a convention, speed dating event, other?) and what would you like to see when you are contacted (sell sheet, overview video, rules, live demo)?**

I always prefer an email. This keeps a record of our discussion. It is best if you contact me with a sell sheet and then also have an overview video for reference.

**What is the best way to contact you (please provide email/form link/alternate contact information)?**

You can contact me at kidstablebg@gmail.com or info@burntisland-games.com

## Publisher

Steeped Games

## Name

Dan Kazmaier

**What are the key things you're looking for when you hear a pitch from a designer (in a sell sheet, in a video, and in-person)?**

Creativity, innovation, or an interesting mechanic that would make someone stop to take a look. We also want to see the designer's passion for their idea, balanced with flexibility as the project comes to fruition.

**What level of prototype would you expect from a designer (in terms of look, art, and polish)?**

Mechanics should be pretty far along with 50+ playtests. Having no art is fine, but to stand out, some placeholder graphics would be preferred as we'd like to see the designer's layout/artistic vision as well.

**Can you walk us through the thought processes as you're looking at a game?**

To be honest, there needs to be a specific hook that really sets the game apart in today's market. We're specifically looking for accessible games for all ages and complexity levels, so the game should feel intuitive as soon as we're introduced to it. We also try to gauge the possibility of expansions right away and consider different themes that might work with the game.

**What are the top three questions that you like to ask a designer when discussing a game of theirs you might be interested in, and what types of responses are you looking for with each of them?**

1. **What makes your game different?**
   We're hoping they can identify something unique that would make their game stand out in today's market.
2. **Why do you feel we're a good fit as potential publishers?**
   We're gauging for compatibility and why they reached out to us.
3. **What's something you'd change about your game right now?**
   We're looking for flexibility, honesty, and a reality check.

**What are the factors that make you most likely to sign a game from a designer?**

Timing is everything. If we have too many projects in the pipeline, it becomes harder to identify something that we can commit resources toward. We need to identify a theme right away that works as well as assess how much development time it will likely take before the game is marketable.

**Let's say a designer has given you their prototype for a game you are interested in. How long should they wait to follow up with you if they haven't heard back and what's the best approach they can take to not come across as pushy or demanding?**

A month is fair, and friendly reminders to check in on us. If possible, it's preferable to know if other publishers are interested.

**How long is your typical production time from contract signing to game release?**

Right now, we're aiming for 1 year.

**How involved do you want a designer to be in the production of the game once the contract has been signed and you have it in your possession? What responsibilities are yours, and which ones are the designer's?**

We'd want the game's mechanics pretty solid before signing a contract, or we'd ask them to redesign that specific area of the game before signing. We welcome as much involvement as the designer would like, but ultimately, we would take the lead in polishing the mechanics, art direction, and graphic design as we're hiring those specialists and marketing. The designer's input is definitely desired, but the responsibility is on us. We'd ask that they are invested in any rule changes and be working with us on future expansion ideas as the project progresses.

**What is the typical type and frequency of communication you have with the designer between signing the contract and releasing the game?**

As development is ongoing, we'd like the designer to be involved as much as they're willing to or able to contribute so that both parties are excited about the final design. We're open about how we work on games, and we'd like the designer to help in this process.

**If you pass on a game, what is your policy or approach about returning a prototype?**

Happy to send it back to the designer or send it to another publisher.

**What types of games are you looking for? What would excite you to see come across your desk?**

We're looking for immersive games where the theme really shines through. It still needs to be accessible for families and have a strategic depth for all gamers to enjoy.

**How do you prefer to be contacted or meet (email, setting up a meeting at a convention, speed dating event, other?) and what would you like to see when you are contacted (sell sheet, overview video, rules, live demo)?**

Speed dating events or email is preferred, though chatting at a convention is also great, but it's hard to schedule a demo. A sell sheet, short overview video, and rules are excellent.

**What is the best way to contact you (please provide email/form link/alternate contact information)?**

hello@steepedgames.com

## Publisher

Grey Fox Games

## Name

Joshua Lobkowicz

**What are the key things you're looking for when you hear a pitch from a designer (in a sell sheet, in a video, and in-person)?**

Core mechanics, player count and play time, and what makes the game FUN.

**What level of prototype would you expect from a designer (in terms of look, art, and polish)?**

Mechanically, the game should be "done." Graphically, it should be playable. Artistically, it should be bare or outfitted with borrowed art. Never pay for anything before pitching.

**Can you walk us through the thought processes as you're looking at a game?**

I consider if any of my brands have a built-in audience. Then I consider if the game has the potential to stand out in the market.

**What are the top three questions that you like to ask a designer when discussing a game of theirs you might be interested in, and what types of responses are you looking for with each of them?**

1. **What makes this game fun?**
   Describe the mechanics or interaction that bring joy.
2. **What makes this game special?**
   Describe how it is different from games with similar themes/mechanics.
3. **How many different people have playtested this?**
   Show me that you have put effort into finding potential flaws in the title and stress that I am not getting a "first draft."

**What are the factors that make you most likely to sign a game from a designer?**

That the game is fun to play, and I think I have an audience for it.

**Let's say a designer has given you their prototype for a game you are interested in. How long should they wait to follow up with you if they haven't heard back and what's the best approach they can take to not come across as pushy or demanding?**

30 days from me taking it to them following up. Sometimes it takes longer for me to get it in the rotation but after a month if they have heard nothing, I am perfectly happy to let them know where it is in the queue.

**How long is your typical production time from contract signing to game release?**

We almost always go the full-term. If it's a 2-year contract, the game generally won't hit until at least 1.5 years after signing.

**How involved do you want a designer to be in the production of the game once the contract has been signed and you have it in your possession? What responsibilities are yours, and which ones are the designer's?**

They can be involved as little or as much as they like.

When it is time to develop a title, I always send a report about how we want to develop the game and the designer can be a part of that process if they want or they can let us handle it in-house.

Truly, once the game is signed, EVERYTHING is our responsibility. But the designers can be a part of it if they want to.

**What is the typical type and frequency of communication you have with the designer between signing the contract and releasing the game?**

Emails often. Phone calls rarely. And the communication is zero until it hits the development table. Then it is a lot from the time it does until the release.

**If you pass on a game, what is your policy or approach about returning a prototype?**

Happy to return upon request at designer's expense.

**What types of games are you looking for? What would excite you to see come across your desk?**

I want it all, honestly. If I have an audience for it (middle-weight, thematic OR Deception-style deduction) it's an easier sell. But I always want to broaden the brand so anything fun, and less than 2 hours will be considered. Engine-building goes over well with our testers.

**How do you prefer to be contacted or meet (email, setting up a meeting at a convention, speed dating event, other?) and what would you like to see when you are contacted (sell sheet, overview video, rules, live demo)?**

Email first with a sell sheet, video after if it might fit, convention meeting or submitted prototype after that.

**What is the best way to contact you (please provide email/form link/alternate contact information)?**

josh@greyfoxgames.com

# Publisher

Lucky Duck Games

# Name

Filip Milunski

**What are the key things you're looking for when you hear a pitch from a designer (in a sell sheet, in a video, and in-person)?**

Type of game, unique aspect of the game (how the game is different or what it does better than similar games already on the market), and target group.

**What level of prototype would you expect from a designer (in terms of look, art, and polish)?**

Clear graphics, no art. More important is how advanced the development is.

**Can you walk us through the thought processes as you're looking at a game?**

1. Does it fit our publishing line?
2. Does it seem to be developed enough and seriously playtested?
3. Is there any unique value?
4. What's the theme and is it strong enough and not pasted on?
5. Does the manufacturing cost look reasonable?

I ask myself these five questions in this particular order. If I have two or more "NO" responses, I do not even ask for a prototype.

**What are the top three questions that you like to ask a designer when discussing a game of theirs you might be interested in, and what types of responses are you looking for with each of them?**

Questions 2, 3, and 4 from the previous section. I expect answers: yes)

**What are the factors that make you most likely to sign a game from a designer?**

It is quite a complex mix. The most important though is do I have a clear vision of a product after my first contact with the game.

**Let's say a designer has given you their prototype for a game you are interested in. How long should they wait to follow up with you if they haven't heard back and what's the best approach they can take to not come across as pushy or demanding?**

I am always trying to set up a deadline when taking a prototype to have a clear picture of the situation and so that the designer knows when he/she can push for the answer.

**How long is your typical production time from contract signing to game release?**

Usually up to 1 year.

**How involved do you want a designer to be in the production of the game once the contract has been signed and you have it in your possession? What responsibilities are yours, and which ones are the designer's?**

I prefer to work closely with a designer on the development of the game, rules, and playtesting. We keep the author informed about all production and art aspects and ask him/her for approval, but it is our responsibility.

**What is the typical type and frequency of communication you have with the designer between signing the contract and releasing the game?**

It depends. During the development, usually frequent, every week.

**If you pass on a game, what is your policy or approach about returning a prototype?**

I prefer to set this up when I take a prototype. If it is important for the designer, we usually send prototypes back.

**What types of games are you looking for? What would excite you to see come across your desk?**

We look for middle weight games with very strong themes and story-driven games with a possibility of app augmentation. I look forward to being surprised by the prototype.

**How do you prefer to be contacted or meet (email, setting up a meeting at a convention, speed dating event, other?) and what would you like to see when you are contacted (sell sheet, overview video, rules, live demo)?**

Mostly via e-mail and meeting at Cons. An overview video is the best option, followed by a sell sheet and rules.

**What is the best way to contact you (please provide email/form link/alternate contact information)?**

filip@luckyduckgames.com

# Publisher

Fireside Games

# Name

Justin De Witt

**What are the key things you're looking for when you hear a pitch from a designer (in a sell sheet, in a video, and in-person)?**

I want to get enough information to really understand what the game is about and to try to get an idea of how it might feel to play. It's important to nail down all the essentials like playtime, components, number of players, etc., but after that, I'm looking to see how it actually plays.

**What level of prototype would you expect from a designer (in terms of look, art, and polish)?**

I may be old school, but I'm actually fine with really rough prototypes. Clip art, placeholder images, paper components, it's all fine. It leaves the game a bit raw, which helps you to appreciate the gameplay, which is what I am actually evaluating. I don't like highly polished prototypes because they can really influence the perception of the theme. If it's a theme that doesn't work or isn't a good fit for our brand, it makes it much harder to see beyond that and evaluate the parts that do work. Also, bad art is a turnoff, so it takes more mental effort to look past a shiny, almost final game with bad art.

**Can you walk us through the thought processes as you're looking at a game?**

My first take is almost a "gut" take. Does this idea appeal to me in any way at all? It could be the name, the theme, something in the description, or maybe a mechanic. I'm looking for a connection to draw me further in as a player. This is also where I look for any obvious red flags.

We get so many pitches that I don't need to explore a game that is not going to work for our brand. So, that could be an issue with too many components for our price points, too much player vs. player (PVP), obviously adult or offensive themes, or theme mismatches (we can't sell war games or sports games).

If a game gets past that first decision gate, then I take a closer look, hopefully at a video to start getting an idea for what the game really is and how it plays. Here is where I try to read past all the sell sheet and marketing language to see what the game really is. I'm looking for how much fun the game is and what it's like to experience it as a player. Does it immediately remind me of something else? Does it jump out as being fun at first glance? Is it confusing to understand as it's being played? Does it look boring or exciting? We are very picky, so if there's a spark of interest there, then it's usually time to ask for a prototype or print and play so we can try the game out ourselves.

If I'm able to demo the game, then my first playthrough is purely as a player. I turn off as much of my designer/business brain as possible and just try to absorb the experience. Am I having fun? Do I understand the rules? Do I think I could get better if I played again? Would I play this again? Those are the core questions I ask myself as a player, so if a game passes all four, then I put on my designer/business hat and do another layer of analysis. Is this game unique enough to stand out in today's very crowded market? Do the mechanics fit the theme? How finished is this versus how much more work does it need? Does it need all the components it has now, or does something need to change? If it was published as is, what kind of price point would it have?

Sadly, I've played tons of "good" games that don't have any real problems but are just not interesting enough to publish that we've passed on. That is purely because of the economic reality of the industry right now. With the volume of games being released, there is very little room for "good" games anymore. They have to be "great."

**What are the top three questions that you like to ask a designer when discussing a game of theirs you might be interested in, and what types of responses are you looking for with each of them?**

My questions are tuned to the game itself, so I don't have any kind of script I follow. The basic ones involve things like are the designers open to theme or art changes, who else have they shown this to, and any possible gameplay changes.

**What are the factors that make you most likely to sign a game from a designer?**

Primarily, how good the game is. That's the core of it all. After that, how flexible they are with changes, schedules, etc. I try to get a sense of what they might be like to work with and avoid anyone that seems too demanding or unrealistic in their expectations.

**Let's say a designer has given you their prototype for a game you are interested in. How long should they wait to follow up with you if they haven't heard back and what's the best approach they can take to not come across as pushy or demanding?**

That's a tough one. It kind of depends on the time of year. We get so busy with convention season that if I get a pitch in May that needs more analysis, I may not be able to get it to the table until after GenCon in August. It is also based on internal schedules, production timing, etc. We're a small studio though, so that will vary a lot from publisher to publisher. Realistically, we try to get prototypes to the table as soon as we can. Really, we don't want to wait longer than a month after receiving them before we respond.

I'm fine with follow-up emails that politely ask how it's going. Sometimes that will catch me at the right time and move it up my priority list, or at least allow us a chance to update the designer on where we are in our process.

**How long is your typical production time from contract signing to game release?**

There is no typical time. I've had some go from pitch to published in less than a year, while others have taken over 2 years. A lot depends on how much development is needed after signing the contract, but really it comes down to fitting the new game into the production schedule. We are always working on multiple projects that are in different states of completion, so anything new is most likely going to move to the back of the line.

**How involved do you want a designer to be in the production of the game once the contract has been signed and you have it in your possession? What responsibilities are yours, and which ones are the designer's?**

We really don't like to sign a game unless it is finished or incredibly close to being finished. In this case, we will update the designer on any changes we make and show them art along the way, but there isn't really a need for a lot of involvement for the most part. Any design changes are done by us, but with the designer as involved as they want to be, and sometimes may even be handed back to the designer to complete. Art, production, and final components are all our responsibility.

**What is the typical type and frequency of communication you have with the designer between signing the contract and releasing the game?**

Back-and-forth emails, while we are evaluating the game, are very common. Rules questions, possible gameplay changes, etc. Once we've nailed down the design and are onto production, communication becomes about sharing art updates, possible cover designs, etc., which are much less frequent. Updates on final release information and any promotions we are doing are the last stage as we get close to launch.

**If you pass on a game, what is your policy or approach about returning a prototype?**

I know how much work prototypes take, so I always offer to return a prototype at our cost.

**What types of games are you looking for? What would excite you to see come across your desk?**

I get the impression that a lot of publishers have a list of game types they are looking for, but we don't work that way. I'm not looking for any particular mechanic or game style, rather I want to have a great experience. I want to be excited by a great theme meeting great mechanics in a way that I haven't seen before. I want to feel engaged while playing. I love it when I actually feel like I'm doing whatever the game is about. I want to have a story to talk about when the game is over, not just a score.

**How do you prefer to be contacted or meet (email, setting up a meeting at a convention, speed dating event, other?) and what would you like to see when you are contacted (sell sheet, overview video, rules, live demo)?**

We attend speed dating events from time to time and those are always entertaining, but most of the games we've signed have actually come from pitches that were sent to us directly. Email is probably the best, with the first message including a sell sheet, rules, link to a video, and any other "demo" type materials. The video is really helpful at that early stage. A link to a print-and-play isn't bad but isn't really necessary at that point.

**What is the best way to contact you (please provide email/form link/alternate contact information)?**

info@firesidegames.com

## Publisher

Gamewright

## Name

Jason Schneider

**What are the key things you're looking for when you hear a pitch from a designer (in a sell sheet, in a video, and in-person)?**

Ease of learning, engaging and unique game mechanisms, and family accessibility.

**What level of prototype would you expect from a designer (in terms of look, art, and polish)?**

A prototype doesn't have to be polished; it just needs to be able to clearly convey the core game mechanisms. The fun should shine through the rough materials.

**Can you walk us through the thought processes as you're looking at a game?**

I wish I had a simple process to walk through. Mostly it comes down to figuring out if the game has that certain Gamewright "je ne sais quoi." Some of that is its ability to be enjoyed equally by kids and adults. I've found that to be a tough formula to design games around.

**What are the top three questions that you like to ask a designer when discussing a game of theirs you might be interested in, and what types of responses are you looking for with each of them?**

1. What was the inspiration for your game?
2. What have been some of the responses from blind tests?
3. Why do you think your game makes a good fit for our line?

**What are the factors that make you most likely to sign a game from a designer?**

The game has to get very strong marks from our intensive playtest sessions with parents and kids. It also has to meet certain requirements for manufacturing and sales margins.

**Let's say a designer has given you their prototype for a game you are interested in. How long should they wait to follow up with you if they haven't heard back and what's the best approach they can take to not come across as pushy or demanding?**

2–3 months.

**How long is your typical production time from contract signing to game release?**

There's quite a range, but it averages about a year from contract to release.

**How involved do you want a designer to be in the production of the game once the contract has been signed and you have it in your possession? What responsibilities are yours, and which ones are the designer's?**

I'm highly collaborative with inventors, even though we take on the entire production. I usually ask the designers to weigh in on rule tweaks, as well as participate in playtests of the games as the artwork is developed.

**What is the typical type and frequency of communication you have with the designer between signing the contract and releasing the game?**

98% of communication is by email. Frequency varies depending on the complexity of the game and how much input is needed during the development process.

**If you pass on a game, what is your policy or approach about returning a prototype?**

If the inventor provides a return address, we send back the prototype. Otherwise, we destroy it.

**What types of games are you looking for? What would excite you to see come across your desk?**

Games that can be enjoyed equally by kids and their parents.

**How do you prefer to be contacted or meet (email, setting up a meeting at a convention, speed dating event, other?) and what would you like to see when you are contacted (sell sheet, overview video, rules, live demo)?**

Most people contact me by email and send digital pitches. I occasionally look at pitches at conventions, but the most successful pitches tend to come via sell sheet, rules, or video demo.

**What is the best way to contact you (please provide email/form link/ alternate contact information)?**

submissions@gamewright.com

# Publisher

Analog Game Studios

# Name

Richard MacRae

**What are the key things you're looking for when you hear a pitch from a designer (in a sell sheet, in a video, and in-person)?**

I'm always looking for something that's unique and stands out creatively, either in the way a game is played or in its theme, but most important is the commercial potential of the game; it needs to have a market.

**What level of prototype would you expect from a designer (in terms of look, art, and polish)?**

It can be useful to review a very well-developed prototype but many changes will likely be made during the game's development, and so, this will inevitably change. Reviewing a very "primitive" or basic level prototype is actually quite fun because it means that if we select the game, we get to be more involved in the creative process of developing the game for manufacturing. In other words, all "levels" of polish are acceptable; it's up to the designer on this one.

**Can you walk us through the thought processes as you're looking at a game?**

First, I need to understand how the game works, then I'll evaluate whether the game is enjoyable to play. There needs to be a fair degree of player control, as opposed to luck. The game needs to fit with Analog Game Studios' product portfolio, in terms of position, which in our case is broadly defined as "Casual Games." The game cannot be longer than a 1-hour experience and preferably 30 minutes, but less is fine too. Finally, and most importantly, there needs to be a defined market segment and commercial channel for the game to be successfully sold in its market and I'll look for this critical factor to be answered through the uniqueness of the game and market that it will attract.

**What are the top three questions that you like to ask a designer when discussing a game of theirs you might be interested in, and what types of responses are you looking for with each of them?**

I'm interested to know why the designer created their game and what they envisioned for its contribution to board games/card games. Since this is open-ended, I'm simply looking for an honest response. Secondly, I'd like to know the level to which the game is developed. Here, I'm looking for insight on whether it's complete and blind playtested or if it's still in development, and where the effort is currently being applied. Finally, I'd like to ask the designer what degree of "openness" there is in making changes or being involved in the game's development for commercialization—the more a designer wants to be involved in the development, the more flexible and easy to work with they'll need to be. Ultimately, it is nice to have the designer stay involved during the development phase since this is their game and we prefer it to be as close as possible to their vision as is commercially possible.

**What are the factors that make you most likely to sign a game from a designer?**

If the commercial potential is high, the game has features that are very unique or creative and different from what has already been published, there is a high degree of enjoyment and entertainment from playing the game, and the designer is good to work with.

**Let's say a designer has given you their prototype for a game you are interested in. How long should they wait to follow up with you if they haven't heard back and what's the best approach they can take to not come across as pushy or demanding?**

Six weeks is good and an email that simply asks how the review is proceeding, unless, I've given a date when I'll get back to the designer, in which case an email the day after that is totally acceptable.

**How long is your typical production time from contract signing to game release?**

It ranges from 6–18 months.

**How involved do you want a designer to be in the production of the game once the contract has been signed and you have it in your possession? What responsibilities are yours, and which ones are the designer's?**

I think I touched on this above, but to recap, the involvement of the designer has a lot to do with the designer's interest in being involved and their willingness to accept changes, and the ease with which they work in a team during the development phase.

**What is the typical type and frequency of communication you have with the designer between signing the contract and releasing the game?**

Major milestones or developments are communicated as they occur through email, with minor news likely found on social media, as we tend to develop games rather openly to the public.

**If you pass on a game, what is your policy or approach about returning a prototype?**

If the designer would like the prototype returned, we will ship it to them. We know that prototypes can be expensive to produce. All designers offer to arrange for the return shipping in these circumstances.

**What types of games are you looking for? What would excite you to see come across your desk?**

Games that excite me are truly novel in how they play and have a very unique theme that can be developed into a beautiful game with a great table presence. The simpler the game is to learn to play and the more complex the options are to the player, with minimal luck involved, the more such games push the envelope in the direction of introducing a truly novel game for the largest number of potential future gamers.

**How do you prefer to be contacted or meet (email, setting up a meeting at a convention, speed dating event, other?) and what would you like to see when you are contacted (sell sheet, overview video, rules, live demo)?**

A sell sheet and/or the rules by email or through our website contact form is a very good start.

**What is the best way to contact you (please provide email/form link/ alternate contact information)?**

https://analoggamestudios.com/form/

## Publisher

Smirk and Dagger Games

## Name

Curt Covert

**What are the key things you're looking for when you hear a pitch from a designer (in a sell sheet, in a video, and in-person)?**

Imagine the back of the box it will eventually have. It should have a broad-stroke overview of the game theme and core mechanics. The number of players, age, play length. But most importantly, in that description, what is the hook that leaves me excited and interested to learn more. Designers know where the fun lies in their game and what has excited players about it, by watching their reactions and listening to their comments after playing. They know what interesting decisions or key features they've built into the design that makes it stand apart. This is all first-level marketing. Make it part of your pitch. I want to know WHY people want to take your prototype home with them after playing. (And if you aren't getting that reaction, it may not be ready to pitch). If it isn't obvious, tell me who the target audience is for the game (players who love X game or X types of games). And do know the company you are pitching to and the types of games they typically make. Sell sheets and videos can be very helpful and show professionalism.

**What level of prototype would you expect from a designer (in terms of look, art, and polish)?**

The prototype needs to be playable. It greatly helps if enough testing has been done to tighten the language for clarity, as well as a strong enough graphic layout to make the game easy to play and understand. These aspects will impact game flow and perception of the game. Do not spend money on illustrations. They will likely be redone, so it is a waste, and any publisher worth their salt can see through that to the design of the game. The only exception is if the illustrations are a core mechanic of the game. Printing the game through someone like GameCrafter does make it feel finished, but you will end up making so many changes along the way, it is often better not to. Card sleeves and color print outs are cheaper and just as effective for presentation.

**Can you walk us through the thought processes as you're looking at a game?**

I wear several "hats" as I look at a game, as a consumer, a marketer, and representative of my own unique brand. First, I am primarily looking as a consumer. Have you piqued my curiosity with your description and overview? Does it sound compelling enough to want to know more? And if we play, am I enjoying the experience? Has it engaged me mentally or emotionally? Does it have a compelling narrative or dramatic arc that makes it feel like we are building to a conclusion? What aspects are most interesting (or frustrating)? Is the expectation of the game's promise, as described in your overview, being delivered in the mechanics and experience of play? (this is important) I observe the other player's faces and reactions - are they engaged?

Assuming this is all positive, does this feel like a game that makes sense for MY brand, or does it feel like someone else's game? If it feels like it's my brand, how easy is it to sell my fans on it? And what aspects make me think so. I will do a rough budget of what it will cost to make the game, estimate how much it would need to sell for, and weigh the experience against the price to see if it feels right. Would I want to buy this game?

If I ask for the prototype to review, this same analysis is applied every time I test it. But the biggest barometer for evaluating "go/no go" is this: Am I consistently getting a spontaneous reaction that indicates people want to own the game? Without asking, "Do you like it?," I am looking for someone to ask, "Dude, when is this coming out?." If that happens regularly enough, I am far more likely to sign the game and publish it (and designers should really not start pitching the game until their own playtests demonstrate this very thing).

**What are the top three questions that you like to ask a designer when discussing a game of theirs you might be interested in, and what types of responses are you looking for with each of them?**

If they have not provided answers to the above already, I start by asking: Who is the audience for this game and what makes them stop and take notice before sitting down? (This sets up the prime audience and sales hooks for that particular audience.)

When people are done playing and get up from the table, what are they talking about?

If they call someone over to take a look, what do they say about the experience that they "have to see this game"? (This is a second way to identify sales hooks and often gets to the heart of what makes the game unique to play.)

Answers to these questions are critical, if not already clear by a designer's presentation.

But here are three others:

1. **How long have you been working on the design/amount of playtesting done/and who have you playtested with (friends and family—or—complete strangers)?**
   This sets the context for how far along in the development process they are. Designers often try to pitch a game that is not yet ready. A game should have received extensive playtesting and revisions with multiple groups that have no connection to the designer, and of the correct target audience.
2. **What type of feedback have you received and are there any areas that you feel need additional work?**
   Very often the designer is showing me a game that is still a work in progress. They may have recently thought about changes or received input that will impact the design. The answer will confirm suspicions I may have or highlight aspects I hadn't seen during the play. This identifies what work yet needs to be done in the designer's eye, layering onto my first impressions.
3. **Who else have you pitched to and what kind of feedback have you received?**
   This helps me understand how deep in the process they are, who they felt was an alternate good home, and provides additional perspectives when they are shared. Or sometimes I learn that I am their first stop, their first choice of publisher, or have been referred by another publisher, which often happens.

**What are the factors that make you most likely to sign a game from a designer?**

Mentioned above, but: Compelling hook, gameplay that meets or exceeds expectations set by the pitch, and it feels like a brand fit.

**Let's say a designer has given you their prototype for a game you are interested in. How long should they wait to follow up with you if they haven't heard back and what's the best approach they can take to not come across as pushy or demanding?**

I typically outline response time in rough terms, so likely not until then. It may be that I will be traveling a lot or have other schedule conflicts, for example.

But I'm fine any time after that. A month is not uncommon to get a first blush response to a design. I don't consider it pushy, so long as it is business-like.

**How long is your typical production time from contract signing to game release?**

This can vary. I have turned a game around in as little as 6 months from signing to a year and a half. Other companies can hold games much longer, which I prefer not to do. But in my case, it is often due to further development that needs doing, art needs, finding the best launch window for the game, etc.

**How involved do you want a designer to be in the production of the game once the contract has been signed and you have it in your possession? What responsibilities are yours, and which ones are the designer's?**

This varies greatly from company to company and typically is impacted by a company's size. Even at Smirk and Dagger, this has had a range. But I typically want to involve the designer in the development and evolution of the game. After all, I'm a game designer too, and they have handed over their baby to my care.

Of course, I need to reserve the right of making final decisions that I feel will help the product and make a strong return on my investment, but no one is served if the designer is unhappy with the changes or surprised by them. Designers know their game best and will be more likely to see problematic impacts of any changes. Of course, they can also recognize mechanics or art decisions that take the design in places they hadn't considered and are delighted by.

So, I make it a habit of notifying them of areas I have marked for improvement. Sometimes they will get excited and work further on it. Other times, I will develop the ideas and present it to them. Either way, I prefer a spirit of partnership. But it is not strictly mandatory.

I also like them to see where I am taking the art and graphics. In the end, once the contract is signed, the responsibility for the product becomes mine. But I encourage designers to be part of it.

**What is the typical type and frequency of communication you have with the designer between signing the contract and releasing the game?**

There is no hard and fast schedule but it is typically by email and at times that seem pivotal for development.

**If you pass on a game, what is your policy or approach about returning a prototype?**

Prototypes are the property of the designers and I always make an effort to return them. I pay for the shipping, of course. Sometimes the design has changed enough that the designer doesn't need the old version back. I have even forwarded prototypes to other publishers for consideration with their blessing instead of just sending them back, particularly if I really enjoyed the game but felt it was not a perfect fit for me.

Designers should not be bashful about asking for them back if it takes a while. I certainly have gotten caught up and have not been as quick to do so as I'd like.

**What types of games are you looking for? What would excite you to see come across your desk?**

I'm open to a lot of games, but the ones that most excite me are deeply thematic, where the theme and the mechanics are woven together tightly. I like the game to be immersive in that theme. I never want to be just pushing cubes. I like a dramatic arc and enjoy games that make me feel something while I play. To be emotionally evocative in some way. I want the memorable moments of the game to be recounted as stories about the experience of play as though we lived it.

**How do you prefer to be contacted or meet (email, setting up a meeting at a convention, speed dating event, other?) and what would you like to see when you are contacted (sell sheet, overview video, rules, live demo)?**

Email is often best, with a brief overview and the hook of the game in text. If it is interesting, following up with a sell sheet, video, rules or live demo is great. I like to do this prior to meeting at a convention, but I have certainly taken the time to do so with people walking up to the booth with a compelling 30-second "napkin" pitch.

**What is the best way to contact you (please provide email/form link/alternate contact information)?**

smirkanddagger@gmail.com/Curt Covert

## Publisher

Tasty Minstrel Games (TMG)

# Name

Seth Jaffee

**What are the key things you're looking for when you hear a pitch from a designer (in a sell sheet, in a video, and in-person)?**

I'm generally looking for something that catches my interest. Vague, I know, but that's just the way it is. I've seen and played a LOT of games, and especially now with so many new games coming out, a pitch has to really excite me before I get too interested.

A game has to EITHER do something new and novel (and also feel like more than a clever idea quickly mocked up into a passable game), or it has to do what it does BETTER than what's already out there. Not every game has to have some brand-new innovation, but a new combination of tried and true ideas can make for a novel game experience. I'm also interested in a game that's like one of my favorites, only markedly better.

**What level of prototype would you expect from a designer (in terms of look, art, and polish)?**

People say a prototype doesn't have to be pretty, which is true to an extent but if you're trying to sell your game (or even get testers excited to play it), then it behooves you to make it look clean and clear.

I do not recommend buying art, but I do recommend spending a little time with Google Image search.

I do not recommend hiring a graphic designer, but I do recommend putting some thought into how the final version of the game will look.

**Can you walk us through the thought processes as you're looking at a game?**

- What games does this remind me of? Have I seen this before?
- What was the designer going for with this rule/mechanism?
- Is there an easier way to do what this rule/mechanism is trying to do?
- Does it feel like this game was thoroughly tested?
- Am I enjoying the process of playing this game each turn?
- Do I feel like I'm making progress?
- Can I determine what progress looks like?
- Are the decisions I'm making interesting, or do they feel like busywork?

- Do I feel like I want to try this again to see if I can do better, or to try another strategy?
- Am I having fun?

**What are the top three questions that you like to ask a designer when discussing a game of theirs you might be interested in, and what types of responses are you looking for with each of them?**

1. **How long have you been working on this game?**
Trying to get an idea of how much playtesting and iteration the game has gone through. Games often (though not always) get better with time.
2. **I'll sometimes ask about common development tricks, such as "have you tried fewer rounds with more starting resources."**
Trying to get an idea of how much development has gone into the game, or if it's basically just an idea and the main mechanism.
3. **Can this game support an (N+1)th player?**
Trying to see how flexible the design is for the player count.

**What are the factors that make you most likely to sign a game from a designer?**

1. The game has to grab my interest with some kind of mechanical hook (and maybe a thematic one as well, though it's usually easier to change theme than mechanics).
2. I have to see some potential in the game—how it could be awesome.
3. I have to see how our audience can look at the game and see good value.
4. The game has to be able to hit an appropriate price point for the perceived value.

**Let's say a designer has given you their prototype for a game you are interested in. How long should they wait to follow up with you if they haven't heard back and what's the best approach they can take to not come across as pushy or demanding?**

I recommend friendly emails, no more than one per month (maybe give a few months at first, especially if the prototype was taken from a big convention like GenCon or Essen, or during con season). After some time (3–4 months if you haven't been getting responses, maybe more if you have been corresponding), higher frequency is probably called for. If they don't even write back, then that's a bad sign. If they respond quickly but just aren't getting to your game after 4–6 months, and you want to pitch it elsewhere, then feel free to ask for it back.

I wouldn't worry too much about coming across as pushy unless you email too frequently. If it's just a reminder that you're out there and that we have your game, then it doesn't seem pushy to me.

**How long is your typical production time from contract signing to game release?**

Probably about 1–2 years. Things always take longer than you think. Sometimes things fall into place, and the lag is much lower, but it takes several months to get art, do pre-press with the manufacturer, print, and ship games, so at a minimum it's probably 6 months if there are zero delays.

Add in time for development, quoting, finding an artist, con season, and getting a chance to evaluate the game in the first place, and it's easily a year or more. If there's a crowdfunding campaign involved, that can add another couple of months to prepare and run, plus potentially more time after the fact to take care of art and graphic design changes created by the campaign.

**How involved do you want a designer to be in the production of the game once the contract has been signed and you have it in your possession? What responsibilities are yours, and which ones are the designer's?**

As a developer, I tend to keep the designer in the loop for development changes, and I (perhaps foolishly) expect them to participate in that process (test changes, work with me to develop their game).

As for production, I do not think that's the designer's scope. It is helpful (and it behooves them) for the designer to help with things like proofreading rules and looking over soft proofs, and promoting crowdfunding campaigns or the game's launch, but I don't see that as their responsibility.

**What is the typical type and frequency of communication you have with the designer between signing the contract and releasing the game?**

When doing heavy development on a game, I tend to send long development emails after playtest sessions (sometimes weekly while actively testing) to keep the designers in the loop and look for feedback from them about proposed changes.

Other than that, there really isn't much communication with the designer. I try to remember to send pieces of art so that they can see their creation coming to life, but that's rare. I do respond to questions, but I don't initiate communication (outside of playtesting) unless I need their feedback.

**If you pass on a game, what is your policy or approach about returning a prototype?**

My policy is that I'll happily return a prototype at the designer's expense.

If a game has a lot of pieces, or rare/expensive pieces, that a designer wants back, then it may be worth requesting a return. Most prototypes aren't really worth the shipping to return them, so many designers don't ask for the prototype back.

**What types of games are you looking for? What would excite you to see come across your desk?**

This might be the most common question, and the hardest to answer.

I'm looking for games that look fun and interesting to me, that have some mechanical (and maybe thematic) hook that makes them stand out, and that I think will excite our audience and have the chance to catch fire like Azul or Wingspan.

I can't really reduce that into a specific list of attributes, it's more like, "I'll know it when I see it," which I realize isn't too helpful.

**How do you prefer to be contacted or meet (email, setting up a meeting at a convention, speed dating event, other?) and what would you like to see when you are contacted (sell sheet, overview video, rules, live demo)?**

Email is probably the best. When I'm at a convention, I'm usually busy with one thing or another. Setting up a meeting at a convention is probably best for in-person pitches.

A sell sheet, rulebook, and maybe an overview video are all very helpful. Photos of the prototype setup are nice for me as well.

**What is the best way to contact you (please provide email/form link/alternate contact information)?**

TMG's submission page is at playTMG.com/submissions, but we're not really taking unsolicited submissions at the time of this publication, so designers should check our website.

## Publisher

Weird Giraffe Games

# Name

Carla Kopp

**What are the key things you're looking for when you hear a pitch from a designer (in a sell sheet, in a video, and in-person)?**

The general things I'm looking for are player count, time, age range, component count, main mechanics, and the hook of the game or why the game is unique and fun.

**What level of prototype would you expect from a designer (in terms of look, art, and polish)?**

The prototype should be understandable and able to be played. It doesn't have to have great art, but enough graphic design that it doesn't get in the way of me enjoying the game.

**Can you walk us through the thought processes as you're looking at a game?**

The first thing I really want to know is why this game is great. If it has anything that makes it stand out or if it's something that would blend into all the other games on the market. If there are mechanics that are unique or different or just not used often together, that's always a plus.

The theme can also be really important, depending on the game. I love thematic games and games with themes that stand out, so that's also something great to see.

If a pitch is geared towards me, that's wonderful. Whenever I get a pitch and the designer tells me why they're pitching specifically to me, I'm much more likely to continue looking at the game instead of moving on to the next one.

**What are the top three questions that you like to ask a designer when discussing a game of theirs you might be interested in, and what types of responses are you looking for with each of them?**

1. **I always ask designers a question about changing their game, like how do you feel about changing the theme?**
   This gives me a bit of a feel for how it would be to work with them. If they respond well to the question, that's great! If they completely shut down, that's not such a good thing. I'm perfectly fine with someone

disagreeing with me and if they respond in a cooperative way that makes it seem like they can be reasoned with and that they can collaborate. That's exactly what I'm looking for.

2. **I like asking about how much the designer wants to be involved with the game after it's signed.**
   I like working and collaborating, so I'm looking for designers that want the same and don't just want their game to be signed and to move on to another game, without supporting the brainstorming and development of the game until it's published.
3. **I also like to ask how often they playtest, as I'd love to work with designers that are willing and able to get the game developed on a schedule.**
   I'd love it if most designers had a way to playtest weekly or more, but if they only playtest once a month or every few months without a good reason, that's a red flag.

**What are the factors that make you most likely to sign a game from a designer?**

The game itself has to be great and do something that really makes it a fit for my company or if I can see the way it could be a game that could make it a great fit, that works as well. How the designer treats me and how much they seem like they'll help the game become a great game that will fit into my product line matters a lot as well.

**Let's say a designer has given you their prototype for a game you are interested in. How long should they wait to follow up with you if they haven't heard back and what's the best approach they can take to not come across as pushy or demanding?**

I usually tell them my timeline and when I expect to have the game playtested. If I don't, I will tell them when they ask about the game. Emailing when I say I should have playtested is great. It gets pushy when someone emails every week, especially when there's a lot of conventions going on. If I haven't gotten back to you and it's been three weeks, it's fine to send another email.

**How long is your typical production time from contract signing to game release?**

It depends on how finished the game is, what other games I currently have signed and if there's better timing for the game. I use Kickstarter, so my shortest time between signing and launching a Kickstarter campaign has been around

4–5 months, but I've had other games signed for 2 years before launching. With some games, they've been a lot more ready, but I wanted to wait for the right time of the year, so that game was pushed off for a year to hopefully have a great launch. From Kickstarter to the retail release, that can be anywhere from 6–12 months, depending on art, development, and manufacturing issues.

**How involved do you want a designer to be in the production of the game once the contract has been signed and you have it in your possession? What responsibilities are yours, and which ones are the designer's?**

I like having the designer super involved after the contract has been signed. I love discussing the game and its issues, as well as trying to maintain the ideas that the designer wanted while also making it into more of a product. It's great when the designer can playtest and come back to me with feedback and even update the prototype. I do like to be able to update the prototype, as well, as I tend to playtest a bit more than most designers and thus get more feedback and things that need to be fixed.

For responsibilities, it's rather fluid from a development standpoint and changes from designer to designer with what they're willing to do and have time for. I do really like it when the designer can help with the marketing of the game, either by helping demo, taking interviews or just posting about the progress on social media.

**What is the typical type and frequency of communication you have with the designer between signing the contract and releasing the game?**

I might talk to the designer every week or even every day, depending on whether I'm at conventions or traveling. I use Slack for Weird Giraffe Games, so if I have any questions, thoughts, feedback, whatever, I can just message all the designers I'm working with and try to get progress made as soon as possible. I do try to talk to them at least every week so that we're all on the same page with what needs to be done and who is doing it.

**If you pass on a game, what is your policy or approach about returning a prototype?**

If the designer has asked for their prototype back, I generally send it back, though I do try to meet them at conventions to lower the shipping cost. If a designer doesn't ask for the game back, their games are usually recycled, and the bits added to all my other game bits if a certain amount of time has passed.

**What types of games are you looking for? What would excite you to see come across your desk?**

Different, easy-to-understand games that have depth to them. A twist on a classic mechanic is a great fit for my line, especially if the game has quick but impactful turns. Low component count is great, as I like to make games that are under $40.

**How do you prefer to be contacted or meet (email, setting up a meeting at a convention, speed dating event, other?) and what would you like to see when you are contacted (sell sheet, overview video, rules, live demo)?**

An email with a sell sheet is best, but it's also nice to have some sort of interaction before this happens. I run the company's social media accounts and go to a lot of conventions, so you have a way better chance of me playing your game if you take the time to interact before contacting me about pitching a game.

Even if it's just to stop by our booth at a convention, say hi, and demo a few of our games, it makes a difference as it shows that you're not pitching your game to every publishing company out there. You've chosen my company to pitch to for a reason and if you've done that, chances are your game is a better fit for me than the people that are willing to pitch to each and every company that they find.

**What is the best way to contact you (please provide email/form link/alternate contact information)?**

contact@weirdgiraffegames.com

# Section V

# Getting Your Foot in the Door with a Publisher So You Can Get Your First Game Signed

# 23

# How to Prove to a Publisher That You're Worthy

> I always ask designers a question about changing their game, like how do you feel about changing the theme? This gives me a bit of a feel for how it would be to work with them.
>
> **– Carla Kopp, Weird Giraffe Games**

You've done a bit of research, narrowed your list, and found just the right publisher to pitch your game to. You've just submitted your game to that publisher you'd love to work with and you're feeling good.

A few days pass, then a few weeks. The weeks start to stretch into months. That feeling of dread settles in.

Did they get my submission?

Did I give them everything they need? Do they hate my game?

It doesn't have to feel this way. You just need to follow a few simple steps that will dramatically improve your chances of impressing that publisher.

## Why It's So Important to Follow Instructions

Most publishers have a specific process they want game designers to follow when submitting a game. Each publisher may take a different approach.

Actually, hold on. Let's take a step back.

The first thing you need to know is whether that publisher is currently accepting game submissions. Note that this can change over time. One day a publisher is open to submissions, the next day they have their submission

DOI: 10.1201/9781003334828-29

form closed down, as they have a pile of games they haven't even begun to evaluate.

So, the first step is to ensure the publisher is accepting submissions. This should be pretty clear on their website. If they're not accepting submissions at this time, move on to the next publisher.

Now that you've confirmed that the publisher will take outside submissions, carefully read over their process. They may outline what types of games they're looking for, and sometimes even what they don't want to see. Save yourself and the publisher a lot of time by only submitting your game if it would be a good match.

Understand their submission requirements and make sure you have everything they need before you submit your game. Some will require a sell sheet, overview video, and/or rules.

Some may ask for a description of the game. This is where that elevator pitch you created will come in really handy.

It's very important to follow a publisher's process. This is where a lot of games are weeded out before they even have a chance. If a publisher sees that you can't follow a simple process, they won't want to work with you.

So, make sure to follow this process step-by-step and include everything the publisher requires.

## Make It Compelling

You only have one chance to make a good first impression.

Make your submission both intriguing and personalized. Your mission is to get the publisher's attention so that they will want to either meet with you to demo your game or request a prototype so they can evaluate your game further themselves.

So, take your time to craft your wording and make your submission stand out above everyone else's.

## What to Include

If the publisher's website simply says, "submit your games to this email address," you should do just that.

But what do you include?

First, make your email personal. If you like or own other games from this publisher, it couldn't hurt to mention this.

You should mention why they will love your game, why you'd love to work with them, and why your game will fit well with their catalog.

Just make sure not to send the same generic email to each and every publisher. No one enjoys a boring form letter. So, put a little effort into wowing the publisher. You'll be glad you did!

It's important to include your elevator pitch, along with your sell sheet and an overview video, unless the process says otherwise.

In your message, thank them for their time and let them know you would be glad to answer any questions they may have about your game.

## Following Up

Sometimes you won't hear back from a publisher for a while. Or at all. It's inevitable.

Publishers are really busy. They have Cons to attend, games they are releasing, other games in development, plus they may receive hundreds, if not thousands of game submissions every single year.

You don't want your game lost in the shuffle, but at the same time, you don't want to come across as pushy.

Patience is the key.

If you submitted your game through a form and there is no other contact information, you may just have to wait.

However, if there is a way to contact the publisher, follow up two to three weeks after you submit your game.

But… And this is a big but… Don't go asking them if they've had a chance to look at your game and what they think of it right away.

Instead, send a nice email politely reminding them that you submitted your game and ask if they have any questions.

This is a good approach that comes across as helpful (because that's what you're genuinely trying to be—helpful), not pushy or desperate. A publisher will often reply to you letting you know that they haven't had a chance to look at your game, but will also thank you for the reminder.

As I said, publishers are busy people, so sometimes a gentle, kind reminder, is all that it takes, and they will often appreciate that you've taken the time to remind them.

## Take Action

Go to the website for the top publisher on your list and review their process. Make sure your game is a good fit for them and that they are currently taking submissions. If it's all systems go, then submit your game, following the steps they've outlined. Make sure to personalize your message and word it in a way that would make you want to learn more if you were the one reading it.

Now, repeat the process for the other publishers on your list. Be patient, and follow up in two to three weeks with those you haven't heard from.

# 24

# When to Send a Prototype and When You Should Never Send One

> No amount of research and preparation can make up for a game that's not ready or an attitude that signals you won't be easy to work with.
>
> **– Elizabeth Hargrave**

So, you've reached out to publishers and found one who is interested in your game.

That's awesome!

Just don't be too eager. You have to pace yourself and make sure you're doing things in the proper order.

Wouldn't it be terrible to spend all that time and effort to get your prototype just right, and then send it out to a publisher with such high hopes, only to have it sent back to you, unopened?

I won't let this happen to you. Read on to discover the steps you need to take next.

## Don't Be That Guy (Or Gal)!

Here's a big mistake that some new designers will make. They find a publisher they like and send them a prototype. This is something you want to avoid at all costs (and it will get costly to ship your prototypes all over the place as well!).

DOI: 10.1201/9781003334828-30

Never under any circumstances should you send a prototype to a publisher unless they have asked for it first. Unsolicited submissions will just get sent right back to you. Or you may just never hear from this publisher or get your prototype back.

It's only when a publisher specifically **asks you** to send them your prototype that you should proceed. Otherwise, you're just wasting your time and money, not to mention hurting your future relationship with this publisher.

## What to Include

Now, if a publisher does ask for a prototype of your game, there are a few things you'll want to include in the box.

First, your game. Well, duh! Of course, you need to send them the actual game, but when you do, double-check that you have absolutely everything included. Go through your list of components (which you should have detailed on your rules) to ensure you haven't missed anything.

Speaking of rules, make sure to include a copy of your rules as well. Remember to review this one more time to make sure everything is there and in the right order so that the publisher will be able to easily understand how to play your game. If they can't figure out how to play your game, they won't play it. And if they don't play it, they won't publish it.

Make sure to include some form of contact information. It can be a business card, or better yet, a sticker on the inside of your game box with your name, email, and address. That way the publisher will remember who this game is from and be more easily able to return your game to you later, if necessary.

Make sure to pack your game well inside a larger box with plenty of cushioning. This will help avoid it being damaged in transit.

## Print and Play

It's also possible that a publisher will request a print-and-play version of your game if it is small and simple enough.

If your game is just 18 cards, it's faster and less expensive to just email a PDF that the publisher can print, cut, and sleeve if necessary.

So, make sure to have a print-and-play version of your game that you can readily email a publisher if requested.

## Take Action

Get your prototype ready. Check that you have all the necessary components and that your rules are up-to-date and explain how to play your game without any issues.

Once a publisher requests that prototype (or you're asked to do a demo), you'll be ready to go!

# 25

# Setting Expectations

> What you're actually pitching is for them to take home a prototype, but the actual selling of the game is something the game has to do on its own.
>
> **– Asger Harding Granerud**

You've sent your prototype to a publisher and you're sure that they're the perfect fit for your game.

So why are you only hearing crickets?

Why haven't they sent you a contract to sign your game?

It can be difficult to play the waiting game and quite often you'll have to do just that when you're waiting to hear back from a publisher.

But there are ways to greatly reduce the uncertainty and any anxiety you might be feeling.

## Make Sure You Know What to Expect

If a publisher requests a prototype of your game, it's very reasonable to ask them about their timelines and set expectations upfront.

When you hand a prototype over to a publisher, ask them how long they estimate they will require to evaluate your game and respond to you about whether they would like to proceed or take a pass. This might be a matter of weeks, or months, depending on the publisher and how busy they currently are, including their backlog of games they have yet to evaluate.

I strongly suggest having an agreement in place, preferably written, that states the length of time the publisher has to evaluate your game before

DOI: 10.1201/9781003334828-31

making a decision. You don't want to do this in a pushy way, but in a manner that respects your time and theirs, and that allows the publisher enough time to evaluate your game properly (remember, your game will be going into a queue behind any other prototypes they have already received).

I've handed off prototypes to publishers, then never heard from them again. Despite emailing them numerous times (usually around 1 month apart, so as not to overdo it), sometimes I never heard a thing.

Publishers are busy. I get it. But to never reply, whether I was sending a helpful email to ask if they had any questions about the rules or asking them if they have any feedback, can be very frustrating. I would rather hear a flat-out "no, we'll pass" than hear nothing at all. That's why having an agreed-upon timeline can be so helpful.

## Why Setting a Deadline Is So Important

You want to agree to a deadline with the publisher for multiple reasons.

First, it gives them some sense of urgency to get back to you within a reasonable time. If they don't get back to you within this time, you can and should follow up, but if they don't act upon this, you know you can move on.

Second, this allows you to pitch your game to the next publisher on your list much sooner if the first publisher takes a pass.

Third, it will save you time and sanity. Rather than having to continuously follow up with a publisher, not knowing where they stand, you can save yourself time. It will also counter that feeling of not knowing where you stand.

By approaching this subject now, you'll at least have an idea of how long the process will take and when you can expect an answer. So, instead of creating a trench in your living room from all your pacing back and forth, you can calmly continue to work on other games and projects, fully knowing when you expect to hear back from a publisher.

## Following-Up by Email—How to Get a Response

But what if the publisher has only requested some further information, such as rules, or that overview video that you created?

I'd recommend giving a publisher two to three weeks before you contact them again. But rather than questioning them about whether they have looked at what you sent, simply send a follow-up to ask if they have any questions about the rules or your game in general. This will often prompt them to reply to you sooner.

Now, what if you sent your prototype to a publisher who requested this, their timeline has passed, and you've heard nothing back from them?

In this case, I would wait a week past the time they said they would reply and send a polite follow-up email to see if they have any questions or feedback on your game.

Once again, this will prompt them to get back to you more quickly, and they may even thank you for the reminder (I've gotten thanked for following up on multiple occasions).

I've included follow-up template emails I've used to get positive responses from publishers in the bonuses section for this book: tinyurl.com/bgbonuspage

## Give Them Time

As I mentioned previously, publishers are busy people. Aside from all the conventions, development work, and other tasks that go along with publishing games, they often receive hundreds, if not thousands, of game submissions every year.

So, they're a bit busy, to say the least!

It's fine to follow up with them if a timeline has passed, you haven't heard from them in a while, or they haven't replied to an email or question.

Just remember that they are people too. Treat that publisher as you would want to be treated.

Be kind, considerate, and helpful.

Build your relationship so you can have a future with this publisher.

## Instead of Getting Defensive, Do This Instead (You'll Thank Me Later!)

The harsh reality is that you will receive more "no's" than "yeses" when you submit your game to publishers. They may only sign a few games out of the hundreds of submissions they receive every year, so don't feel bad.

It's kind of like applying for jobs. You may send out dozens of resumes, receive a handful of interview requests, but only get one or two job offers.

Eric Lang, Matt Leacock, and Reiner Knizia have all had games rejected.

Think about that for a moment. Even the greats hear "no". Probably more often than not.

Whether it's game design or anything else, everyone has to deal with rejection. What's most important here is how you react to that rejection.

Do you throw a fit?

Do you tell the publisher that they'll be sorry they didn't sign your game?

Or, do you thank them for their time and ask for their feedback on how you could make your game better or if they know of another publisher that would be a better fit?

You can see that the last approach is by far the most effective. Even if they reject your current game, if they see you as a designer with potential who will be good to work with, you now have a publisher who will be more willing to look at your future games.

Also, keep in mind that publishers talk. They know which designers are good to work with and who they should avoid like the plague. And, they let other publishers know.

Your reputation is important. Always keep this in mind.

## Take Action

If you've been in touch with a publisher, whether it was a pitch, sharing rules that they requested, or they are evaluating your prototype, don't hesitate to follow up with them in two to three weeks. Just make sure to do so in a helpful manner, asking if they have any questions. Use the template here to help you get started, then adjust the wording for your game and the appropriate stage of review: tinyurl.com/bgbonuspage.

# 26

# What Do You Do If a Publisher Says No?

> I'm watching the designer to see how they react to questions, critique, suggestions, commentary. Defensiveness is not a great sign but it's not necessarily a dealbreaker.
>
> – **Paul Saxberg, Roxley Game Laboratory**

It's inevitable. Sometimes a publisher will say no.

It could be for any number of reasons. It might not even have anything to do with your game. In fact, they could love your game, but it just doesn't quite fit with their plans.

So, what do you do if a publisher says no?

## What Happens to Your Prototype?

I've been very fortunate. Every publisher whom I have sent my prototype to has at least offered to return it to me. In some cases, I have said "yes, please!" and thanked them graciously for doing so. In other cases, especially when it was just a deck of sleeved cards or a small game with nothing included that I didn't already have readily available, I thanked them for the offer, but let them know it wouldn't be necessary.

Prototypes can be expensive. You may have put a lot of time and effort into putting this together and may have spent hundreds of dollars. There may be only one or two copies in existence.

So, it may be very important for you to be able to get this prototype back.

DOI: 10.1201/9781003334828-32

However, shipping can be expensive. Even more so if it's going to another country.

You can't always expect the publisher to offer to send a prototype back to you if they take a pass. If you want your game back, you may want to offer to pay to have it returned. The publisher is under no obligation to return your prototype to you (unless you've already agreed to this otherwise) and it would put them out of pocket, so if it is crucial for you to get your prototype back, offer to pay for this yourself if the publisher doesn't.

If a prototype isn't that important to you, then don't worry about it. The publisher may recycle the parts, just as you would do with a cheap game you may have found in a thrift store.

However, if you have another publisher who is also interested and would like to evaluate your game, you could always contact them to confirm they are still interested, get their address, and ask the original publisher if they could mail it to them at your expense. This will save you the cost of having it shipped to you, then to another publisher.

## Don't Get Your Hopes Up Too High

You may walk away from a meeting with the publisher feeling really good. They may even take a prototype of your game right then and there and be talking about how well it would work with their current lineup. You may be pumping your fist and eagerly anticipating a contract for your game.

I encourage you to be cautiously optimistic. Remember that nothing is final until you sign on the dotted line. And even then, it's not *really final* until your game is on the shelf.

Things can change. A publisher may find a game that's even better suited to them at their next meeting and only have enough space to add one more game to their queue. They may like the game initially but repeated playtesting might lead to concerns about replayability or being able to sell enough copies.

I've been there. What was supposed to be a sure thing turned into a polite decline. The publisher went so far as to ask for the prototype right away and asked that I did not show it to any other publishers and said they would have given me a contract right then, but didn't have any of them at the moment. That sounds like a sure thing, right? Well, a few weeks later after they had played the game with their gaming groups, they changed their minds.

But I was also able to turn this into a long, very positive relationship with a publisher that I am regularly in contact with about my games and development.

This publisher is always interested in seeing what I have in the works and it will just be a matter of time before we find a project to collaborate on together.

So, stay positive. Keep working with and communicating with a publisher, making any necessary adjustments to the game. Just don't go tell everyone you know about the game you're about to sign until it is a sure thing. The disappointment of rejection stings more when you have to tell a lot of people that this just isn't happening after all. I know. I've been there!

## Now's Your Chance

Ok, so a publisher has taken a pass on your game. No big deal. The reality is you'll hear "no" way more than you'll hear "yes." It's a sheer numbers game. If a publisher receives 500 submissions and only puts out five games in a year, then 99% of the games they see will be rejected.

But you have an advantage. If you've been following the steps in this book, you have a game that's much further developed than most, you've targeted the right publishers, and you have a solid pitch, sell sheet, and video to promote your game. So, your chances have already improved dramatically.

If a publisher says no, this is a perfect opportunity to ask for feedback. Thank them for taking the time to evaluate your game and ask if they have any feedback or advice about your game. It may turn out that they have another game that's too similar in the pipeline. It may just not fit with their current lineup. Or, they may have discovered some flaws in your game that you'll definitely want to know about.

If they say your game is great but just not a good fit for them, this is also a great chance to ask them if they know of another publisher that would be a better fit. Publishers talk. Many know each other and what types of games they're looking for. If they see you've been good to work with and open to feedback, they may be able to guide you toward a more suitable publisher.

There's also a lot to be said for being nice. Even if things don't work out with the current game you have been discussing with a publisher, if you've had a good rapport, they will often be very interested to see other games you're working on in the future.

The last thing you want to do is get angry or make a big deal out of this. Just let it go. There may be another publisher out there that's an even better fit for your game. Sometimes these things happen for a reason. It's also much easier to pitch new games to a publisher you already know and likes you rather than one who has never met you.

Networking and building relationships with others in the industry, especially publishers, will pay dividends. They can get you in touch with other publishers who might be looking for a game just like yours, or you may create another game in the future that is a better fit. Having your foot in the door with a publisher is a major advantage.

## Take Action

If you have a game rejected by a publisher, be sure to thank them for their time, and ask if they have any feedback to make the game better. Offer to pay to have it shipped back if you need it, otherwise, let them know they can keep the parts. If you have another interested publisher, follow up with them and see if you can arrange to pay to have it shipped to the next publisher on your list.

# 27

# Peanuts and Promises—How Board Game Designers Get Paid

> The great part is that the journey is incredibly fulfilling even before you reach the destination.
>
> **– Emerson Matsuuchi**

I see this question come up from time to time—just how do board game designers get paid?

So, I'd like to get into this and clear up any misconceptions out there.

First off, the title of this chapter is meant to be comical. Of course, we don't actually get paid in peanuts or promises, but sometimes it may feel that way!

There are very few game designers who can make a living doing this full-time without any other source of income. They always say that it's hard to make a living designing games due to the payment structure, long development timelines, and uncertainty. You just never know when your next game will get signed, how many years it will take after that before you see your first nickel from it, or if your game will do well (or even see the light of day!).

I'll start by saying there is a distinction between freelance game designers and game designers who work in-house at a game publisher. I'm the former, as are most game designers, so I will focus most of my attention here on freelancers.

## In-House Game Designers

I will start with a quick piece about in-house game designers. Like in most companies, this position would be paid either by the hour or the individual would be on salary. You'd take home a regular paycheck just as you would in most jobs.

DOI: 10.1201/9781003334828-33

Some of the larger publishers have their own staff of game designers, whereas with a really small publisher, and I'm talking where this is a one-man/one-woman show or it's run by a couple of people, the owners may do everything, including game design. But many of the small to medium publishers (as well as some of the larger publishers) look outside their walls to find game designers with great games.

## Freelance Game Designers

This is where freelancers come in. Freelance game designers create games on their own and pitch them to publishers in hopes of getting their games signed. If a publisher likes what they see in a game and are interested in working with the designer, they will take a prototype and do further playtesting. They may or may not ask the designer to do some more development work, but ultimately, they will make the decision whether or not to sign the game.

By signing the game, I'm referring to the process of the publisher offering a contract to the game designer for the rights to the game. This is also known as a licensing agreement. Once the details have been ironed out and the designer signs the contract with the publisher, typically they will be paid in royalties.

## Getting Paid—How Royalties Work

So, let's say you've signed your first game with a publisher. Congratulations! That's awesome news. But how and when will you see any money from this?

Each time a copy of your game is purchased, a percentage of this sale will go to you. But don't worry, you won't be receiving cheques for $0.12 every other day. Instead, these royalties will be banked up and paid to you regularly, according to the agreement in your contract.

You can expect most publishers to pay this quarterly, usually within 30 days from the end of the quarter. However, some publishers have different pay schedules, such as twice per year. The publisher should also be able to provide you with details on the number of sales of your game each period, and you should ensure this is outlined in your contract.

How much you earn from royalties depends on the details of the contract. Typically, publishers will pay from 4% to 8%, but keep in mind that most base this on the wholesale price of the game, not the retail price. The wholesale price of the game is normally 40–50% of the retail price.

So, what would that mean for you? Let's say your game was sold in retail for $40 and your agreement pays you a royalty of 5% on the wholesale price. Let's say that the wholesale price is $20 (50% of the retail price). That means you'd receive $1 for every game sold (5% of $20). If they managed to sell 1,000 copies that quarter, you could expect a $1,000 royalty cheque for those 3 months.

But what if your game sells next to no copies or the publisher changes their mind and decides not to produce your game (keep in mind either of these scenarios can definitely happen)? Well, you might have been lucky enough to receive an advance against royalties, also simply referred to as an advance.

## What the Heck Is an Advance?

An advance means that the publisher will pay you upfront some set amount of money for the right to be able to publish your game. Now, keep in mind that this is an advance **against royalties**, so you will have already received your payment of royalties based on some set number of game sales.

Let's look back at the previous example to show how this works. Say your publisher gives you a modest $700 advance against royalties. In that first quarter, 1,000 games were sold, netting you $1,000 in royalties. But you've already received a $700 advance, so the first $700 of these royalties was already paid to you upfront. That means your first royalty cheque would actually be $300. You still made the same $1,000, you just got most of it in advance. The good news is, even if they only sold two copies, you'd still get to keep the $700.

Now, keep in mind that not all publishers provide an advance. This is usually limited to larger companies with a much bigger budget. If you sign on with a small publisher and your game will only be their second game to go to Kickstarter, don't expect anything upfront. They will be running the campaign to gauge interest and gather the capital necessary to get the game manufactured in the first place.

But that doesn't mean you can't or shouldn't try to include an advance in your contract. I'd highly recommend discussing this with any potential publisher, and I'll show you how you can do this in a way that is a win-win for both you and your publisher in the upcoming chapters.

You may also be fortunate to have a publisher pay you a small amount to hold onto your game for a longer evaluation period. You may have an agreement with them that they have 3 months to review your game, but if they need more time then they will have to compensate you for this. Again, this is more likely to happen with a larger publisher as opposed to a smaller one. However, you'll want to set limitations on how long they can hold your game as well. If they take forever to get back to you and then eventually pass on your game, you may be missing out on an opportunity with another publisher.

## Other Alternative Payment Methods

While the arrangements above are the most common, you may also meet some publishers who offer you a different method of payment. In particular, a small publisher who is just starting out may want to have you more involved in the project to have more hands on deck, as running a Kickstarter or otherwise getting your game published can be a lot of work.

They may agree to share some portion of the profits with you, at least for the initial print run. Or they may make some other arrangement. This could be more profitable for you but may also take more of your time.

Think of all this as a primer for contracts. In the next chapter, we're going to get into the nitty-gritty details of your contract to ensure you get the best possible deal and that both you and your publisher are happy with the agreement you're about to enter into.

## Take Action

Now that you have an understanding of how you'll get paid as a game designer, let's dive deeper into this in the next chapter and talk about what to look for in contracts and what to avoid to ensure your first game won't be your last.

# Section VI

# Contracts—Understanding What's Important to You

# 28

# Knowing If This Is Really the Right Publisher for You

Research publishers. Look at their catalog, read what their website says about what they're looking for, and listen to podcasts they've been on. Target the ones that actually fit your game.

**– Elizabeth Hargrave**

Ok. You've found a great publisher and they really love your game. In fact, they love it so much that they want to sign an agreement to publish it.

But how do you know that the contract they provide you with is in your best interest and doesn't contain any loopholes that you will later regret discovering?

## It's Ok to Ask for Help

First off, I want to say that I'm not a lawyer. Nor am I a contract specialist.

The information provided here is based on my own experience as well as the experience of other game designers who have been kind enough to share their thoughts with me. This is not a replacement for professional help.

If you receive a contract from a publisher, especially your first one, my best advice is to consult with a lawyer, particularly one who is familiar with the board game industry or at least royalty contract arrangements, to ensure that your rights are maintained.

It can also be helpful to speak to other more experienced board game designers who have been through the contract process multiple times. They will know what to look for and what you'll want to steer clear of.

DOI: 10.1201/9781003334828-35

They will often even be willing to read over your contract and let you know if there's anything that is concerning or that has been left out that you really should include.

There are plenty of board game design groups online, including Facebook groups such as The Board Game Design Lab and Card & Board Game Designer's Guild. Just take note that many publishers also frequent these groups, so be cautious about any specific details that you post. It's best to reach out to other designers you know, or if you don't know a lot of other designers, you can always ask if any experienced designers would be willing to review the contract with you. Make sure to first block out any details that you might not be comfortable sharing (your address, anything else personal to you).

## Give Me All the Juicy Details!

Congratulations! You've received your first offer to get your game published! You should be excited. But you also need to think with a clear mind.

Many new game designers jump at the chance to sign their first game with a publisher. Any publisher in fact and with whatever terms the publisher is offering, even if these terms are terrible.

But you may not know any better. It's going to be your first offer, which will be followed up by your first contract. You're going to be really excited at the thought of getting your game onto store shelves and may be too eager to agree to whatever the publisher is offering.

This can be a huge mistake that you'll later regret. But it definitely doesn't have to be. Let me help you to make sure you don't make that same mistake.

## What Is Their Reputation?

When a publisher shows interest and wants to sign your game, quite often they will first discuss the terms with you before they present you with a contract, just to make sure you are both on the same page.

Before agreeing to everything, make sure you do your homework. If you've been following the advice in this book, you will have already researched publishers and found those who are the best match for your game.

But you'll also want to know more about that publisher and their reputation before you agree to anything. This is when a little research can go a long way.

If the publisher uses Kickstarter, check their history. How many games have they launched? How many of these were successfully funded? Were they able to re-launch failed campaigns and meet their new funding goal? Is the number of backers on each of their projects trending upward?

If the publisher prefers going directly to retail, look at the popularity of their other games. How do they rate on Boardgamegeek? Do you see a lot of their games on store shelves? What games of theirs have you played? Do they use high-quality components or does it feel like they took the cheap way out?

Also, find out what other people are saying about this publisher. The most ideal situation would be to ask other designers who have worked with them to share their impressions. It's easy to look up a publisher's catalog and find out whose games they have published.

## What Are the Expectations (Large vs. Small Publishers)?

You might have a very different experience with a large publisher vs. a small publisher.

A small publisher, especially a one-man or one-woman show, might be doing this part-time. As a result, they may ask for more of your help. This may involve further development, blind playtesting, demoing your game at different events, and supporting a Kickstarter campaign. You may also have more say in the art and general direction of the game than you would with a larger publisher.

A large publisher, on the other hand, will likely have a team to handle everything. You may hand off your game to them and they will do all the rest. They may ask for your opinion on certain things, but don't expect this. It will likely be less work for you once the game is handed over, but this is at the expense of your involvement and creative control.

Whatever the case may be, discuss with the publisher what expectations they have of you in advance. Know how much more work you may need to put in and how involved they would like you to be in the project.

Many publishers I've worked with and talked to have responded to the question of how involved you want a designer to be with "as involved as they choose to be." So, quite a few will be glad to have you involved, within reason. But remember, as the publisher, they do have the final say.

## What Are the Timelines for Publishing Your Game?

It's also good to ask what the timelines will be for your game.

Will they be running a Kickstarter for your game within the next 6 months? Will it be added to their queue and take another 2–3years to be released?

While the publisher won't be able to give you an exact release date at this time, and plans may change, you should at least be able to get a good idea of when your game will be coming out and how the publisher intends to release it.

## Know What Your Deal-Breakers Are

There are probably certain things that are really important to you when it comes to your game. Know which aspects you're more flexible with and which ones are deal-breakers.

Do you have an aversion to releasing your game on Kickstarter? Do you want to have a say in the creative process? Is there a timeline that's just not acceptable to you?

Remember, the publisher has the final say in everything once you sign your game over to them. They will decide on the look, art, mechanics, and may change the theme or name of your game. It's possible that it could look and maybe even play very differently than the game you handed over.

You have to be ok with this. If creative control is the most important thing to you, then self-publishing may be an option you'll want to consider.

## Take Action

First, make a list of all the things you'd want to see in your contract. This can be related to timelines, creative control, method of selling the game, etc. Now, determine which aspects are "nice to have" vs. deal-breakers.

If you've received a contract, review this thoroughly to see if there are any deal-breakers. Even if you see these in your contract, remember, anything can be discussed and negotiated.

Also, it's recommended that you review your contract with others that have more experience than you, including a lawyer.

# 29

# What to Look for in Your Contract

There will most likely be lots of changes, big or small. A designer must be able to stomach that process.

**– Cody Thompson, Gold Nugget Games**

The contract you receive will likely be many pages long and may contain a lot of legalese. There are a number of details you'll want to look for, which I will go into greater detail on, including:

- The royalty rate
- Advanced payments (if any)
- Terms
- Length of term
- Rights
- Extras (such as free copies and the ability to purchase additional copies at a reduced rate)

Now, we get to the part you've been waiting for. Getting paid!

Most game designers are paid based on royalties. That means that you get a percentage on each copy of the game that is sold. However, this doesn't mean that the publisher will pay you after every sale. That would just be a ridiculous amount of paperwork and cheques flying around!

Instead, the contract will outline the payment arrangements. Typically, you will be paid quarterly or semi-annually, within a set timeline (often 30 days) following the end of this period. A sales report should also accompany this royalty payment.

DOI: 10.1201/9781003334828-36

Royalty rates vary by publisher and designer. They may also be based on either the **retail or wholesale price** of the game, so be very aware of what is outlined in your contract.

Typically, the royalty rate will be somewhere in the ballpark of 4–8% of the wholesale price of the game or 3–6% of the retail price (tinyurl.com/gamecontracts). But remember, this does vary by publisher. Be on the lookout for the exact terms and whether they have based this on the wholesale or retail price, as this difference can be enormous.

So, let's say your game sells for $50 in-store. The wholesale price could be between $20 and $25. You can see that there would be a big difference between earning 5% of the retail price vs. 5% of the wholesale price ($2.50 vs. $1-$1.25 per game)!

Yet, some publishers may make other arrangements, particularly if they are a small publisher and are launching the game on Kickstarter. If the publisher is a one-man or one-woman show, they may need a lot of your help and support to make the game successful, and therefore may compensate you in a different way, such as profit-sharing.

Just be aware that calculating the profit on a game can be tricky. Also, remember that profit = revenue – expenses. So, if that publisher claims a lot of expenses, including art and graphic design, and the full cost of events and travel to conventions where your game was only one of their priorities, that profit may shrink down to nothing.

If your publisher offers profit sharing, my recommendation is to include a minimum payment. So, it could be worded as something like "30% of profits from any crowdfunding campaign or $1,000, whichever is higher." This would be similar to an advance, only you wouldn't get this upfront. However, this would ensure that no matter what, you are guaranteed to get something out of the arrangement.

## Advanced Payments

Some publishers, particularly the larger ones, may offer you an advance payment. This is something that smaller publishers will likely not be able to do, as they may rely on Kickstarter to gauge the demand, and/or may not have the upfront funds to provide you an advance.

An advance payment is just that. The publisher is paying you in advance before any copies of the game are sold. This is often a really good sign, as the publisher is indicating a strong interest in your game and is willing to put their money where their mouth is. It also shows the publisher is likely managing their resources well to have a payment they can offer upfront.

The advance payment may be in the hundreds or thousands of dollars, and you should always be sure that it is stated as a **non-refundable** advance payment. This means that even if the publisher is unable to sell enough copies to pay your royalties up to the amount of the advance payment, they cannot claw any of this back. This money is yours no matter what. Even if the publisher decides not to publish your game or goes out of business, you will receive some form of payment.

The amount of the advance payment will be determined by the publisher and could be based on a set amount that they give to all designers or a set number of copies they would need to sell to cover this payment.

It's really nice to receive a non-refundable advance, not only because it is guaranteed income, but also because it gives a clear indication that the publisher is serious about your game. You won't receive an advance for every game, but it is definitely appreciated when you do.

I will discuss how to go about getting an advance from your publisher in Chapter 31 on negotiating the best deal on your contract.

## Terms

There will also be many terms in your contract. These will relate to your payment schedule, provision of documents by the publisher (records of sales, etc.), currency, expiration of the contract, and others.

There will also likely be sections notifying you that the publisher has complete ownership, along with the right to obtain a copyright. You should also ensure that the contract states that your name, as the designer, will appear as a credit on the game (preferably including on the front of the box).

You'll also likely be asked to warrant that you are the sole owner of the work, you have the power to enter into the agreement, and your game is your own original work. This is to protect the publisher in case of a lawsuit. It may go without saying, but make sure that your game is original and not taken from elsewhere.

## Length of Term

One of the most important aspects of your contract is around timelines. You want to ensure that your contract specifies a reversion clause, that is, that the rights for your game will revert back to you if the publisher does not manufacture or sell your game within a set period of time. This is typically two years but may vary from publisher to publisher. Failing to have this stipulated in your contract will allow a publisher to hold onto your game forever, regardless of whether the game is made or not. Including this stipulation also ensures the publisher is serious about producing your game within a reasonable timeframe.

The amount of time to release the game should be reasonable to both the designer and the publisher. A publisher must be given enough time to complete any development work, obtain art, get the game manufactured and into distribution, or run a Kickstarter campaign and fulfill all the orders if they choose to go this route.

But what is a reasonable amount of time? This can often be 2 years, but I have heard of contracts that can allow the publisher up to 5 years to release the game. Now, 5 years might sound excessive, but this is more an exception than a rule and would be specific to only a small number of publishers. This is something you can always discuss and negotiate when you receive the contract.

You'll also want to ensure there is a clause for the length of time the publisher can retain the rights to the game once it has been published. This is typically based on the length of time from the last print run of the game. This can also typically range from 2–5 years. This is a nice clause to have, as the publisher will give you back all the rights to your game after a set period of time has passed. At that point, you can pitch the game to other publishers, self-publish if you choose, or do further development on the game.

## Rights

When you sign your game with a publisher, you're handing over the rights to it. Once you do this, be aware that the publisher can make any changes that they choose. They may consult you, but they are not obligated to.

You're handing over creative control in exchange for their expertise in getting your game manufactured and out into the world.

Your contract will specify a number of rights that both you and the publisher will have.

Many other rights will often be specified in your contract, including the right of the publisher to produce derivative works (other products) using the same theme or concept, quite often without any compensation to you as the author. There will likely also be a section stating that any derivative works using the same or similar mechanics will provide you with compensation at the same rate as for your original game.

What happens in the case of expansions or spinoffs of your game? Will you hold the rights to create these or can another designer create these and sign them with this same publisher without your involvement or ability to collect royalties on these products?

If you want to maintain control and be involved in the development of any other products in the same line, make sure to discuss this with the publisher and have this stated clearly in your contract.

I know of designers who have been completely involved with every expansion or new version of a game they originally created. I also know of other situations where expansions and variations of the game were created with absolutely no involvement or consent from the original designer. In these cases, the publisher had all the rights and could proceed without any issues.

A publisher may also include a "right of first refusal" on your next game. This will allow the publisher to be the first one to receive a pitch and the opportunity to evaluate and sign your next game before it can be presented to any other publisher.

This is not necessarily a bad thing at all. If you like working with this publisher, then why wouldn't you want them to potentially sign your next game? Of course, there are no guarantees here either way, and your next game may not even be a good fit for them, but with all the challenges that go into trying to find a good publisher for your games, this can be a great opportunity.

However, there are some conditions related to rights and the "right of first refusal" that you will want to watch out for. I'll go into these dicey conditions in more detail in the next chapter, "How to Avoid Getting Trapped in an Exploitative Contract".

## Other Things to Consider

There are many other aspects of your contract you'll want to ensure are present. Here are just a few of them that should be included that you'll want to review:

- How many free copies of the game you will receive

- The ability to buy more copies at wholesale price (your contract should also state that you are allowed to sell these on your website or at events)
- The currency of payment

You may be offered some "extras" in your contract. These may include a set number of free copies of your game and the ability to purchase additional copies at a discount (typically at wholesale price). As with everything else, the number of free copies you will receive will differ from publisher to publisher, but this may be one of the easiest things to negotiate if you want some additional copies.

These free copies will allow you to demo your game, give some out to friends and family or anyone who playtested your game as a way of saying thanks, or you could donate them to a board game café or game store to be used as demo copies. This could get your game in front of more people and potentially generate even more sales.

There should also be a stipulation in your contract to allow you to sell copies of the game on your website and events (quite often this is allowed so long as the publisher is not also selling copies of your game at the same event). You may never choose to do so, but it's nice to have the option.

There are so many other parts of a contract in addition to these above. Some contracts can be 10 pages long (or longer), whereas others will cover everything in just a few pages.

There's a lot to read, understand, and consider.

Take your time with your contract and don't rush. Have others with more experience read this over with you, and strongly consider having a lawyer do the same.

## Take Action

Review all the rights, terms, and conditions of your contract. Determine what is acceptable and what you'd like to negotiate. We'll be getting into the negotiations stage soon.

# 30

# How to Avoid Getting Trapped in an Exploitative Contract

Know why your game fits their line and adds to it.

**– Don Eskridge**

While most publishers are good to work with and just want to produce great games for their audience, you still have to watch out for the odd shady character.

Let me walk you through what to watch out for.

## The Two Words You Do Not Want to See in Your Contract

*A word of caution*: While a "right of first refusal" on your next game can be a good thing, a "right of first refusal" on *every game* or giving away the rights to all your future games to a publisher should make you run for the hills. Most publishers would never try such a tactic but there are a few who will present you with a sketchy contract that either gives away your rights to future games, is full of loopholes, or is intentionally vague.

The two words you never want to see on your contract are: "**in perpetuity**".

What does this term mean? **Unlimited time**.

That means that the publisher will own your game (and maybe all future games, depending on how this is worded and what they have included in your contract) forever. Even if they decide to never publish it, which happens more often than you'd think.

DOI: 10.1201/9781003334828-37

No matter how badly you want to be a published game designer, it's not worth it to sell your soul. Don't do it.

You don't want to work with the kind of publisher that uses predatory tactics and tries to take advantage of new game designers by getting them to give up the rights to future games or your ownership of any of your games forever.

It may be legal, but it is highly unethical and takes advantage of someone who is either overly eager or doesn't know the ins and outs of contracts.

Again, it's best to have more experienced people, including other game designers and a lawyer, review your contract to help make you aware of anything that might be concerning.

## Actual Examples of Concern from Real Contracts

Other game designers were kind enough to provide me with a few examples to share with you of vague wording or other concerns that should give you second thoughts, or at the very least, have you asking for much more clear wording. Here are some examples and what you should watch out for.

### *Example 1—Unusual Designer Responsibilities and Lack of Clarity*

*Development Development is the process of refining the game design before manufacturing. It includes such things as playtesting, design adjustments, theme design, production research, game illustrations, component design, packaging design, writing rules, and budgeting.*

*Where applicable, the Publisher and Designer shall bear the costs of developing the Game. The Publisher shall work closely with the Designer to bring the Game to a publication-ready state.*

The concern with the wording above is that the publisher has indicated that both the publisher and designer will bear the development costs. This is highly unusual. While the designer may be asked to playtest suggested changes, they should not incur any costs related to art, package design, or anything else related to the production of the game. This is the publisher's responsibility. Also, even if this were typical, the contract does not specify how this would be shared.

This is very vague and a bit scary to see in a contract.

*Example 2—Details Intentionally Left Out*

*Licensing* ≪this section left intentionally blank≫

*Final Statement upon Termination* ≪this section left intentionally blank≫

*Disposal of Stock upon Termination* ≪this section left intentionally blank≫

It's really curious why a publisher would intentionally leave a section on something as important as licensing blank, or any section intentionally blank, for that matter. Yet, this was done for not one, but three sections in the same contract.

This would have me asking the publisher to immediately revise the contract with these sections completed so that I could fully understand what I was signing.

*Example 3—More Missing Details*

*Payments and Escalators* *Within twenty-four (24) months following the first sale of the Core Product, an escalator of $####.00 (USD) shall be immediately paid to Creator upon the sale of every #### physical unit of the core product.*

Umm. So, what is the dollar amount and number of units? No, the designer did not blank these out before providing me with the example. This was in the actual contract.

For examples of real full contracts, like the ones reputable publishers use, check out the bonus section for this book: tinyurl.com/bgbonuspage

## Reviewing Your First Contract and Knowing What to Look Out For

It's finally happened. The day you've been waiting for. You received your first board game contract.

You're shaking with anticipation. You can't believe your game will finally see the light of day. And with a real publisher, too!

But you've never signed a licensing agreement before. You have no idea if what they're offering you is good or even if it's fair to you as the one who put in all the work to create your game.

And now you're thinking… Am I getting a fair deal?

Is there anything else I should be asking for? Am I even allowed to negotiate?

I'm a nobody. Not a big-name designer. Should I just take whatever they offer?

These are just a few of the questions that are going to pop into your head as soon as you receive that contract.

Let me help you to navigate these muddy waters so that you don't end up signing your game design soul away.

I also want to preface this again by saying that I'm not a lawyer. I'm talking from my own experiences here. You should always seek legal advice if there is something you are unsure of.

## When to Sign That First Contract (and When to Run Like Hell)

You've reviewed your contract, ensuring you understand all the wording and that the publisher is not trying to pull a fast one on you. But that doesn't mean you have to sign over your game immediately.

What if you were able to get better terms or include something else in your contract that was important to you?

What if there was a way that both you *and* the publisher could share in the rewards together if the game becomes a hit?

Let's talk about how you can do just that.

## The Contract They Present You With Isn't Final

Just because you're a new designer and this is your first contract doesn't mean you have to accept the first offer. You're allowed to discuss the details. You can negotiate the royalty rate, advance, number of sample copies, or anything else in your contract.

If the publisher doesn't budge on one area, see if they are flexible in another area.

If you're just not happy with the contract or some terms are ambiguous and unclear, make sure to speak up. Don't sign anything until you're comfortable with all the wording. Talk to other game designers and have them review your contract to see if there's anything that looks strange or too open-ended.

If the publisher refuses to clarify anything in the contract or you feel like you're being taken advantage of, don't be afraid to say "no" and walk away.

You're better off not having your game signed than being under the control of a publisher who will take advantage of you.

Now don't get me wrong. Most publishers are great. I really do want to emphasize this. There are very few who will outright take advantage of you. But they do exist, so I just want you to be careful, especially when signing your first contract.

## Take Action

Read over your contract closely, watching out for words like "in perpetuity" and rights to future games. Be sure that you are comfortable with all the language used in your contract. If something worries you, be sure to get help understanding the terms. And never sign a contract until you are completely happy with the terms.

# 31

# Negotiating for the Best Deal

> Be pleasant to interact with while working booths for companies. Let designers and publishers know you are a fan of their work. Say thank you to all the people who give you advice, invite you to dinner, or score you a meeting.
>
> – **Eric Slauson**

As I mentioned in the last chapter, the contract a publisher presents you with isn't final. You have the right to negotiate and get better terms.

But you have to do this right. You want to show the publisher you're easy to work with and have each other's best interests at heart. Let's get into how to do this right.

## Increase Your Earnings Over Time

I want to share with you something that I've included in every single one of my contracts that guarantees me more money if my game does well. In some cases, the publisher included this in the contract, but more often than not, I've been the one to bring this up, and in every case, the publisher has agreed. This goes to show that most publishers are willing to work with you to create a fair agreement.

This is something that allows not only me but also the publisher, to earn more from the game. It's truly a win-win situation.

In addition to the base royalty rate, I always ensure the publisher includes **escalating royalty rates**. This means that I will earn a higher percentage from royalties if the game sells more copies.

DOI: 10.1201/9781003334828-38

For example, I might earn 5% of the retail price for the first 5000 units sold, but this will increase to 6% for units 5,001 through 10,000, and 7% for anything above 10,000 units.

It's obvious that I'm getting a better deal when the game sells more copies, but how does the publisher benefit from this?

Well, the cost per game gets reduced when you increase the number of copies manufactured. So, additional larger print runs will often cost less than a small initial print run.

Also, the sunk costs, including graphic design, art, molds, and production samples (as well as any costs related to running a Kickstarter campaign, if the publisher goes this route) are already taken care of, so they won't have to be accounted for in additional print runs.

This is an example where everyone can share in the rewards.

So, this is something you **must** bring up with your publisher. They can set the rates and quantities (although you can also make suggestions—I have and the suggestion was agreed to without a concern), but you need to discuss this if it is not present in your contract. It's a simple matter that if the game does well and they print more copies, they will have paid off any sunk costs and will often be able to print these additional copies for a lower price. The best way to word this is that you are both reaping the rewards for a successful game and partnership.

Check out the email example where I have asked for and received an escalating royalty rate with no questions asked right here: tinyurl.com/bgbonuspage

## Advances and Guarantees

As mentioned previously, you may also be fortunate enough to be offered an advance against royalties. This means that you are getting paid some of the money upfront for the work you've already done.

Even if a publisher doesn't offer you a non-refundable advance, I highly recommend discussing this with them. My suggested approach is to say that you know they are serious about your game and you're confident in their ability to market it well and sell all the copies they produce (and you honestly should be this confident in them if you are signing over your game to this publisher). You've put in the hard work to develop a game that they believe in, so it would be fair and reasonable to include an advance to compensate you for your work and demonstrate their genuine belief in your game.

If you look at the numbers, it all makes sense. Let's say your royalty rate will pay you the equivalent of $1 per game sold. If the publisher is intending to make 5,000 copies (a very reasonable number for a small to medium publisher) or more, they would only have to sell the first 1,000 copies to make up this royalty payment to you. If they're going to get that many copies made, they'd better be confident about selling at least 1,000 of them!

So, if they are going to do so anyway, paying you upfront shows that they are serious about getting your game on the shelves and are willing to pay you a small amount for the work you've already done. Artists and graphic designers get paid upfront, so it would only be fair for you as the game designer to get some upfront payment, even if it is only $500 or $1,000. This rate, by the way, can be anywhere from a few hundred to many thousand dollars, depending on the publisher, game, and reputation of the designer.

This gives the publisher more skin in the game, encourages them not to shelf it, and will ensure that a publisher is serious about your game and their own ability to sell all (or at least most of) the copies they have made in that first print-run.

It's much less likely, but the publisher may even include a guaranteed minimum royalty in the contract. This means that regardless of the number of copies they sell, you will be guaranteed a minimum amount of payment.

Both advances and guaranteed minimums are really nice to have, and they also prove the publisher is serious! Even if the game doesn't sell well, you will have earned *something* for all your hard work.

## Take Action

Check your contract to see if it includes a non-refundable advance, guaranteed minimum payment, or escalating royalty rates. If not, discuss these with your publisher, using the win-win aspects I've mentioned in this chapter.

# 32

# Congratulations! You've Got Your Game Signed. Now What?

> I need to know that a designer is not finished designing when they start working with us. Very rarely does a publisher get a game in their hands that doesn't need development.
>
> **– Helaina Cappel, KTBG/Burnt Island Games**

You've signed the contract and your publisher now owns the rights to your game. You're excited and you should be! This is a big moment and it deserves a celebration. Do something nice for yourself or take your significant other out for a night to rejoice.

But does it just end there?

Is there anything you can do to help your publisher get your game out faster and make it more successful?

Your publisher may have a whole team who will handle everything, but then again, if they are a smaller operation, they could definitely use your help.

## Coming to an Agreement

Once you've negotiated all the details in the contract and both you and the publisher are happy with the result, it's time to sign your contract.

They will likely mail you two copies of the contract, with both copies signed by one of their representatives. You'll sign both copies, keeping one for yourself, and mail back the other copy to the publisher. This way you both have one signed copy of the agreement.

DOI: 10.1201/9781003334828-39

## Understand Everyone's Expectations (Not Just Your Own)

As I mentioned earlier, you should get a clear understanding of what the publisher's expectations are of you.

What will the publisher be responsible for? What will you be responsible for?

Could you help them with further blind playtesting? Development work? Art suggestions?

For some designers, they're happy to just hand over everything to the publisher and let them do the rest. After all, they're the experts, right? But other designers want to help out where they can. They want to see their creation come to life and be more involved. How much help is needed, or even wanted, will be up to the publisher, but most are happy to have you pitch in and share your ideas at the very least.

## Handing in Your Work on Time

One of the expectations the publisher will have of you is to provide them with anything they need to move the game forward within a certain timeline.

At the very least, they will want a copy of your up-to-date rules and any other files related to your game, such as cards, tiles, and any other components used in your game.

Make sure you understand exactly what your publisher wants and when this is due. Get that information or those documents to your publisher on time, or better yet, early. This will show the publisher you are good to work with and can deliver on a deadline.

## Lend a Helping Hand

Sometimes the publisher won't come right out and ask for your help. But that doesn't mean you can't offer.

If you'd like to stay involved, it is perfectly fine to ask if they would like your help with any further development, rules review and updates, editing, or anything else.

Even if they've got this under control, they will appreciate the offer.

## Understand That Your Game Won't Be Out Tomorrow (and Be Ok With That)

If you thought it took a long time to take your game from an idea to a great-playing prototype and get it signed with a publisher, that's just the start.

It can often take a year or two (sometimes more) for further development, art, graphic design, and further testing of the game before it is actually manufactured and on store shelves.

Of course, this depends on the publisher, their marketing method, their backlog of games, and other factors. If they don't have any other games in their queue and are planning to bring your game to Kickstarter as their next project, it just might be out in a matter of months, rather than years.

In any case, you're going to need to practice patience. Hopefully, your publisher will keep you up to date on development, including graphic design and art, and share progress with you throughout the process. They may even ask for your help in developing the game further, testing rule changes, and once again, updating the rules. It's good to mention up front that you would love to be kept up to date as your game develops.

In the meantime, work on more games! You can even start to think about expansions or different versions of the game. If it's a hit, the publisher would undoubtedly love to see more games or expansions in the same world. Remember, publishers are largely risk-averse. If a game is selling well, they're more likely to want to build on this success rather than taking on an unknown game.

## Congratulations, You're a Published Game Designer!

Finally, the day has come. The publisher has your game manufactured and it has arrived on store shelves, bringing happiness to gamers everywhere.

Congratulations! You're now a published game designer.

You've accomplished something that very few have (relatively speaking). It's every game designer's dream to have their game published, and now it's a reality for you.

Celebrate this huge win, then get right back to what you love doing—creating more amazing games!

## Take Action

I want you to take a moment to **imagine what it would feel like** to see your game on the shelf of your local game store. Picture how amazing it would look, with professional art and a gorgeous box. Watch how other people are playing and loving your game. This could be your game one day soon.

Keep reading and discover lots of great advice as well as game signing stories from other published designers in the next and final section.

# Section VII

# Stories from the Battlefield

# Appendix

This section is a collection of advice and stories provided by a number of other published game designers. I hope you find it both helpful and inspirational!

## Elizabeth Hargrave (*Wingspan, Tussie-Mussie*)

Advice for getting your game signed with a publisher:

1. Research publishers. Look at their catalog, read what their website says about what they're looking for, and listen to podcasts they've been on. Target the ones that actually fit your game.
2. Prepare, prepare, prepare. When I went to pitch the game that became Wingspan, I recorded myself over and over on my phone until I wasn't stumbling over myself anymore. I was incredibly nervous, but I knew exactly what I wanted to say and how I was going to show off my components and gameplay. Nerves may have taken my super-polished pitch down to normal person talk but if I hadn't practiced a lot, I would have gone from normal person to stammering idiot.
3. No amount of research and preparation can make up for a game that's not ready or an attitude that signals you won't be easy to work with. Playtest like hell, finish your game and then be prepared to get the feedback that you're not finished and take it with grace and enthusiasm.

DOI: 10.1201/9781003334828-41

## Don Eskridge (*The Resistance, Black Hole Council*)

I was relatively lucky as a first-time designer. I designed *The Resistance* because I enjoyed *Werewolf* but wanted to improve upon it in some significant ways. Once I'd written the rules, I simply published it as a PnP on BGG. Thankfully it caught some attention, and after around 30ish ratings I received an email from Travis of Indie Boards and Cards. He was interested in publishing, and we went on from there.

Although that first experience went well, since then I have approached publishers a number of times in my career. My tips are not so different from what you'd hear from many professionals, and they also are not so different from tips used for successful interviews in general. Anyway though, here are some:

1. **Do regular research about the industry.** Know what other games the publisher has published and be able to talk about them and how they relate thematically or in some other way to yours. Have a functioning prototype ready to show, and most of the time a rulebook ready to deliver as well. It will be clear as you describe the game whether you love it or not. You should if you want it published. Know how to teach it simply and effectively, try to show the interesting moments but also let the game reveal itself. Don't spill your guts. Remain calm, interested, and genuine. Be curious about the publisher's product line, origins, and future.
2. **Know why your game fits their line and adds to it.** Show that your game's components are in line with their budget. Before publishing *Abandon Planet* through my own Orange Machine Games, I approached *The Resistance* publisher about it. He advised that the game's decisions were simpler and more along the lines of a light social game, but that the components were closer to a $50+ game. As a less experienced designer, I ignored this and published the game myself. Although I don't regret publishing two games through OMG, I learned that it's important to let people who are good at something give you advice and learn from it.
3. **Try to create an idea or brand for yourself, in order to make it easier for them to remember you.** For example, I consider my games to be "explosively interactive." I say a number of other things as well, including about ease of learning, feeling of building a story together,

and sense of delight and surprise. Try to build the professional idea of you, along with the game you're pitching, since it's easily possible that they pass on this game but keep you in mind for the next, along with the experience brand you've described.

4. **Being a game designer is a multipronged skill set.** I am a creator, but also an entertainer to my friends when they come to play games at my house (I entertain so that they want to come again). Use that relatability you've learned from play-testing nights with the publisher. I am also a humble graphic designer; nobody will ask you to make professional work, but your prototypes should be clear and reproducible. For at least a decade I've simply used Microsoft Publisher to make my drafts, and these days I'm moving on to Component Studio by the Game Crafter. Game-Icons.net is also invaluable for icons. Use these and other resources to not only make copies of your game but to be ready to show up at a convention and print two entirely new sets if you need to. Keeping this in mind will also inspire you to simplify your draft components for this reproducibility.

## Eric Slauson (*Tattoo Stories*)

I taught 6th grade English language arts for 9 years. During that time, I had a three-part motto that basically covered all of my classroom rules and expectations. That catchall phrase is "**Be there. Be ready. Be kind.**" Instead of delivering a long list of really specific do's and don'ts on the first day of school, I presented this phrase to my new students and we generated a common sense of understanding of how this phrase might apply to our work together as learners, creators, collaborators, etc. That phrase, which has served me well as an educator, has also proven incredibly useful as a game designer. So, instead of listing all the little things that have led to what success I've had so far as a designer, let me explain how these three guiding principles have influenced my behavior and decisions in the industry.

### *Be There*

You HAVE to go to conventions. Okay, maybe you don't HAVE to. Several people have designed games that win online design contests and go on to be published. Some people self-publish and find success entirely through word of mouth and digital marketing. I have found, however, that every single good thing that has happened to me professionally as a designer can be traced back to me attending a convention.

I don't necessarily even mean games I have pitched at conventions that have been the ones signed. None of the games I've signed (at the time of writing this) have actually been the result of a meeting I scheduled at a convention. However, they have been signed because I was at an after-party where I heard someone mention they were looking for a game about X. Or, I was at a prototype event within a convention and a publisher saw the crowd around my table. Or, I played a game with a stranger who happened to know somebody who knew somebody else who was looking for a game exactly like the prototype I was working on.

This is very much an industry of connections. Whom you know is often as important as what you've made and going to conventions is the best way to build those relationships with fellow designers and potential publishers. I view conventions as an essential expense if you want to really get to know the gamers and publishers your product is for.

Not only is the convention itself a great way to play a lot of games, but the dinners, bar crawls, hotel lobby gaming and other "after hours" events have provided incredible opportunities for networking and making great friends. Working for a company at their booth is a great way to offset convention costs, but it's also a great way to practice pitching as you try to sell their games, highlighting the benefits, explaining the mechanics as concisely as possible, etc.

Go to conventions.

As a minor additional point to this, try to "be there" in some digital communities. I'm an active member of several Facebook groups, and those groups have introduced me to a lot of great people, new perspectives, and even some co-designers.

### *Be Ready*

This advice has paid off at pretty much every convention or gaming event I've attended. As a designer, you should definitely have your elevator pitch–a SHORT summary of the hook of your game–memorized. This is really important for capitalizing on when "being there" puts you in the right room with the right person.

The next level of preparedness is having your prototypes on you at all times. I always try to "be ready" at every moment with my most viable prototypes. I wear my backpack around the convention hall, out to dinner, and even out to clubs to go dancing (thank goodness for coat checks and lax dress codes), always ready to pull out a polished prototype or an MVP to show if the opportunity arises.

In my bag are usually one to three full prototypes, containing rules, a sell sheet, and all the pieces needed to play an entire blind playtest of the game. These can be given to publishers in the exciting event that they ask for a prototype to take back to their offices for review.

In addition to these kits, however, I also have 2–5 MVPs or rough drafts that have enough components to play a few rounds or act as a proof of concept but don't really represent what the actual game may become. These rough drafts are useful to have on you for several reasons.

First, they are available for quick playtesting if your group has a few spare minutes between games. Even strangers will usually sit in the open play area for an extra 5 minutes if you explain you just want to see what their thoughts are on a specific mechanic.

Second, if you have a meeting with a publisher to pitch a game, you should always start the meeting by asking, "What are you looking for" and be ready to respond to those desires. The answer to this question usually surprises me (Oh, this party game company is actually looking for a meatier abstract! Hmm, this company that usually makes big box games actually wants to start a new imprint for microgames), but if you have your stuff with you, you might have the beginnings of a game that is just what they are looking for.

### *Be Kind*

Lastly, be kind. This is just good advice for being a person, but there are several ways you can be kind as a game designer. Think of ways you can make your games more inclusive. Help other designers by testing their games. If you don't have what a publisher is looking for, but you know someone who does, try to get your fellow designer a meeting.

Be pleasant to interact with while working booths for companies. Let designers and publishers know you are a fan of their work. Say thank you to all the people who give you advice, invite you to dinner, or score you a meeting. Be kind to yourself by taking care of yourself during conventions and staying mindful of your mental and physical exhaustion.

So, there you have it. Everything you need to be successful as a designer:

**Be there, be ready, and be kind.**

## Chris Chung (*Lanterns, Spell Smashers*)

Nowadays I find it not enough to have a great game. Just like networking to find yourself contacts to grow your business, it's about putting yourself out there and openly sharing your game with people. You don't even have to share your game with publishers yet (that'll come in due time), but ensure you meet up with designers in your area or at conventions because people can always give you a heads-up about who's looking for what games and may help you get noticed. Secrecy is your greatest enemy!

Also, join social media, if you haven't done so already! I signed *Lanterns* because I connected with Randy Hoyt of Foxtrot Games through Twitter.

Stay patient but stay hungry. Publishers often have many games in their pipelines, and your game may not be a fit in terms of their timelines.

If a publisher expresses interest in your game, give them a copy, but don't be disheartened if they can't get back to you within a reasonable time frame. I had to wait a while before hearing back and sometimes I'd drop them an email or message asking them the status. Just don't incessantly bother them. You want to ensure that they believe you're a great person to work with as well, so being a bother won't help your cause.

If you aren't working on multiple games at once, do so! Granted, a good chunk of people are dead focused on one game, and that's fine, but what happens if a publisher likes you but may not like the current game you're pitching enough to sign it? Having a multitude of games will not only impress publishers and show them you're flexible around working with different themes and mechanics, but you're also less likely to be viewed as a one-trick pony.

And who knows? Maybe they'll even like another game you're not necessarily pitching to them in the first place. Randy playtested a game of mine called "Full Metal Contact" and I asked him if he had an interest in publishing it. He asked me if I had anything else, and I had this one called "Blossom" that turned into the *Lanterns* you see today.

## Scott Rogers (*Rayguns and Rocketships, Pantone The Game*)

I have pitched many games to publishers. I have pitched at tradeshows, at speed dating events, and by private invitation. I have had my games signed six times by publishers, with two having been published and a third game that is due out in 2020. While I have pitched my games many times, the stories for each of these games are very different.

My first "sold" game (*Magician's Club*) was picked up by a publisher who sat on it for 3 years. They tried to redesign the game but couldn't come up with anything better than my original design. Eventually, the rights to the game reverted back to me.

My first published game (*Rayguns and Rocketships*—IDW Games, 2017) was originally designed as a video game. However, I realized I couldn't afford to make this as a video game, but that I could afford to create a board game version of it.

I designed and built a prototype, and then I playtested the heck out of the game at conventions and private events. I commissioned the game's beautiful cover art. I photoshopped the cards and the playboards. 3D printing was just starting to become a thing, so I commissioned a 3D artist to create models based on my character designs and had them 3D printed.

I then did my research on which publishers might be willing to publish it. I went to my FLGS (friendly local game store) and wrote down the names of every publisher who made genre games with miniatures. I e-mailed those companies and scheduled 13 pitch meetings at Gen-Con. Out of the 13, three publishers were interested. I ended up going with IDW because they "got" what I was trying to do with the game and there was potential for other marketing efforts based on the license (comic books, toys, and clothing). I later found out that they picked up the game because they loved how professional my prototype looked. They eventually ran a Kickstarter for the game, which funded. *Rayguns and Rocketships* is now available for purchase on Amazon and at your FLGS.

My second published game (*Pantone the Game*—Cryptozoic Entertainment, 2018), I designed very quickly (over a week or two) and through a friend, pitched it to Mattel. They didn't bite.

I was on my way to San Jose Protospiel to pitch another game and brought the game (originally called "Who's Hue?") with me on a whim. At the show, I was talking with a publisher who asked me if "I had a game that could be played in 15 minutes". I showed them Who's Hue? and sold it to the publisher with a hand-shake deal. They ended up not publishing - the party line they planned on making it a part of didn't materialize - and they reverted the rights back with me.

Later in the year, I was attending Gen-Con, once again pitching other games. I was talking with Cryptozoic Entertainment and I almost didn't show them the game—I thought they wouldn't be interested in it. It turns out that they had the *Pantone* license and were looking for a game to go with it. I just happened to show up with the "right" game. Now, *Pantone the Game* is available for purchase on Amazon, Barnes and Noble, and your FLGS.

My third (to-be-published) game was pitched to a publisher at Gen-Con. They liked the design and they seemed nice. I later learned that they were creatively invested in the game. They sent me tons of great feedback from their playthroughs, which proved to me that they wanted to make the game even better. I liked their attitude, their creativity, and their spunk. The publisher just showed me box art last week and the game (*Diamonds and Dinosaurs*) is scheduled to be on Kickstarter next year.

The fourth game I sold was picked up by a relatively new publisher who was eager to make a big name for themselves. They seemed pretty passionate. They wanted to re-theme the game, but they could never quite find a better fit than the original idea (which was a Seance).

Our relationship went all the way to the verbal contract agreement stage, and we were discussing money and rights when suddenly, the publisher backed out of the deal. I found out later that they had other projects they were more interested in pursuing. I don't feel bad about losing the deal—I have other publishers interested in the game—but I think they conducted business rather unprofessionally. This demonstrates why you need to be careful with who you go into business with.

Here is my advice for game developers getting ready to pitch their games to publishers:

- Make your prototype look as professional as you can.
- Do your research and find out what other publishers are looking for.
- Pitch one game at a time, don't overwhelm the publisher, but make sure to bring your other prototypes "just in case."
- Always present your game to a publisher in person. Your enthusiasm for the game goes a long way in getting people excited about it.
- Even though your game gets picked up, that doesn't mean it will get published.
- Never give up. If you are persistent, (and you don't suck) and you want it bad enough, you will eventually get published.
- Get your game out there however you can. If no one will publish it, try self-publishing. The creator of *Uno* sold games out of the trunk of his car before it was published by Mattel.

I hope this helps! Good luck to all of you designers!

## Adrian Adamescu (*Sagrada, Sinister Six*)

### Co-Designing Games

Should I pursue board game design? Could I do it full-time? These were the questions I was asking myself every day a few years ago. There I was, in my mid-30s, having graduated with a Ph.D. in Chemistry and applying for teaching and postdoc positions at the local universities and colleges. So, why would I be thinking about designing games full-time?

To make the matter even more complicated, my wife had recently been laid off and was at home with the kids. So, what is there to even think about? Get a "real" job as quickly as possible! Stop this wild fantasy! Yet, there was that little bit of hope that maybe I could do it.

Two years prior I had met Daryl Andrews, a local game designer who had just signed his first game, *The Walled City*. WOW! A "real" game designer! I had been working on a game myself and even submitted it to the 2014 Canadian Game Design Competition, but having a game signed, now that was a big deal! How could I ever get there?

At the time, Daryl was having playtest nights at his house and I was invited. There would be more "real" game designers there and a few members of the Game Artisans of Canada as well. Should I also bring my game? I had never tested it with anyone other than my wife.

Here's my first advice to aspiring board game designers: The real test, to see if your game is any good, is to get it out there and let it be played by people who don't know you personally. Don't be afraid of their critiques.

They tested it and it was "too long!," but other than that there weren't any major complaints and people seemed to enjoy it. I can still remember a mid-game moment after the dice were rolled and the whole group started cheering. Hmm, I have created a moment. I cherished it. I wanted to create more of those moments!

Fast forward a few months and Daryl and I would meet once a week to share our game design ideas and playtest together. I started taking longer and longer lunch breaks, so I could go print prototypes, cut out cards, and buy the right amount of colored dice. It was at one of these meetings where I showed Daryl the game that would become *Sagrada*.

When I was faced with the question if I should pursue game design full-time or not, I didn't know how *Sagrada* would do long-term. The game had just finished a successful Kickstarter campaign with almost 3,000 backers, which was encouraging, but many Kickstarter hits have struggled with sales after their campaigns ended. In an industry where thousands of games are released every year, it is easy for a game, as hyped up as it may be, to drop from public consciousness in favor of the next big thing.

So, here is my second piece of advice for aspiring board game designers: Don't quit your day job just yet. Although I wasn't finding the teaching position or postdoc I was looking for, I kept tutoring and doing some other part-time work to be sure I could pay the bills.

My last and most important piece of advice has worked really well for me: Find the right person to work with. For me, co-designing games (mostly with Daryl) is the best way to do it. We complement each other in many ways. I'm timid and I don't like crowds, but love math, figuring things out, and doing artsy stuff on the computer, while Daryl loves to attend the big conventions, playtest with a lot of people, and deal with the business side of things. The author of Ecclesiastes said it best: "Two are better than one because they have a good return for their labor."

## Seiji Kanai (*Love Letter*)

To tell the truth, the success of my best hit game *Love Letter* was in 2014 (released originally in 2012 in Japan), and the world of board games has changed completely in the last 5 years or so.

A lot of talented designers have appeared, and there are a lot of very, very interesting games on the market. Crowdfunding on platforms like Kickstarter can provide big money to board game projects, and influencers or famous YouTube talents with hundreds of thousands of followers can use board games to attract others.

So, my method for success may no longer be as relevant. What I would say is I think the most accessible method to succeed is to make games based on recent trends, such as mystery or escape rooms, or easy communication/ice-breaking games, which influencers can easily present in a video.

But there are a lot of veteran designers, newer designers, and interesting titles already published.

So, if I could give any advice, it would be something that is not only relevant to gaming.

It is best to cherish and be honest in your relationships, and with your friends in the gaming world, playtesters, and personal connections for publishing.

Continue to make games. This may not connect to success, but it becomes the power behind designing great games.

Some of my designer friends say that success is just the result of rolling the dice. To have luck when rolling the dice, it's best to be honest in your designs.

## Gord Hamilton (*Santorini*)

I designed *Santorini* during midterm examinations in December 1985. I played it over the next two summers with two fellow summer students: Scott Ursenbach and Diana Kim. From 1987 to 1988 I spent my meager student income to try to get it published. That included printing up several gaudy $600 multicolored boards, stitching together felt bags and scouting out generic circular building blocks. I called the game "Ascent." The boards allowed play on 3 × 3, 4 × 4, 5 × 5, and 6 × 6 squares, depending on which concentric colors you adopted. Not surprisingly, no publisher bit. The first "industry expert" that playtested it sent back a one-sentence critique, "The game should be called 'frustration'."

The next time I pursued this was in the late 1990s when Gigamic short-listed "The Block Game" as one of the top 10 games in 1999 out of a field of 400 submissions. By that time there were about 20 "God cards," but the artwork was mine (horrible!) and the theme was not well defined.

In 2004, I had given up on getting my game published and decided to go it alone. By this time, I had re-named the game *Santorini*. I purchased white blocks from Kamloops, British Columbia, along with white boxes and BIG white elastic bands from ULine. I assembled 160 *Santorini* boxes, each with 8 God cards. The artwork was Greek nudes, which I scavenged from the Internet.

Those 160 games sold out. Of course, I didn't make any money, but I got my idea out there and people liked it. It got a 7.4 average rating on Board Game Geek. Most importantly, it got the attention of Michael van Briesbrook, whose amazing AI was later to enable quick assessment of new God ideas and to critique my old God ideas.

I kept on trying to sell *Santorini* and my other games without success until finally, Family Games America bought the 5-year-rights to publish *Santorini* in 2009. I hired a local lawyer to go through the contract, and he spotted nothing wrong, so I signed. I got no upfront fee, but I wasn't concerned. I was walking on air.

In 2014, *Santorini* had still not been published. Gavan Brown from Roxley games wanted to publish it, so we got the rights back from Family

Games America. The Kickstarter went brilliantly! It made over $700,000! Thirty-one years after the first prototype, it was finally a viable commercial product. This was due to Gavan's awesome aesthetic vision, coupled with the artistry of Mr. Cuddington, and the God-editing skills of Lee Mitchell, Michael Van Biesbrouck, Simon Rourke, and Richard Castle.

Spinmaster then contacted Gavan, wanting to buy the worldwide rights to *Santorini*. The most exciting part of that 8-month negotiation was that Spinmaster discovered that Family Games America had secured the trademark "Santorini." It took $15,000 to get it back. To be fair to Family Games America, they had been manipulated by lawyers who agreed to do trademarking for a reduced fee—but that the trademark was then jointly owned between the law firm and Family Games America so Family Games America did not profit from the whole trademark debacle.

I visited Spinmaster headquarters in New York earlier this year. Great people. What an awesome end to an irritatingly long adventure!

## Alexander Pfister (*Great Western Trail, Broom Service*)

In the end, it's the game that matters. Publishers are looking for the next hit. Of course, they have their own brand, so you should keep yourself informed of what complexity or genre they sell.

Does the publisher only sell party games, light strategy, or family games? Then only show them this type of game.

But also keep in mind that some publishers have an editor or developer, who is willing to playtest and change the game a lot. If you show them a fantastic, yet a little unbalanced game, they may not mind, because they will make changes anyway.

When presenting a game to a publisher, focus on the core mechanism. What makes the game unique? When they test your game, then they will be looking behind the curtain. They will determine what mechanisms are good and what they should change to improve the game.

Other publishers want to invest less time into development, so they are really looking for a finished and balanced game. Presentation and a good rulebook are maybe more important to them than to the first group. They will play your game one time and they need to enjoy the experience. If they like your game as-is, you have a good chance to get a contract. But if they see problems, they might reject the game, whereas the first group of publishers might accept it, because they can identify possible solutions.

So, the conclusion is: The better you know the publisher and how they work, the better you can focus on how to best present your game.

## Phil Walker-Harding (*Sushi Go, Imhotep*)

When I was starting out designing, I entered a few game design competitions. I found this to be a great way to get my work in front of people in the industry, and to get really useful feedback. Many of the competitions around the world are judged by publishers or other designers, and some can even lead to a contract. Two of my games found publishers through this pathway.

In terms of pitching designs to publishers, it seems that most companies these days prefer face-to-face meetings at conventions. I am based in Australia, which is a long way from the industry epicenters of Europe and the USA. But early on, I decided a trip to the Essen Spiel fair was worth it to present some of my designs. I have found that most publishers are very open to meeting, even with relatively new designers. This welcoming atmosphere is a great characteristic of the industry.

My biggest tip for pitching is to spend some time coming up with one exciting sentence that sums up what your game feels like to play. I often start a meeting with this and find it helps orient how the publisher hears the rest of your pitch. I have also found that prototypes with good table presence can really help a pitch. This doesn't mean it has to look like a finished product with professional artwork, but well-sized pieces, bright colors, and good clarity in the graphic design are big plusses that might help the publisher imagine an exciting finished product.

## Emerson Matsuuchi (*Century: Spice Road, Century: Eastern Wonders*)

Being a game designer can be equal parts exciting and daunting. With so many games being released in record volumes and even more designers than ever before trying to get their games into the world, the road to being published is an uphill climb.

The great part is that the journey is incredibly fulfilling even before you reach the destination. There's a lot of work that needs to be done with designing a game, testing, iterating, convincing your friends to help you test it again, revising and iterating again, and bribing/begging/blackmailing your friends to test it again. But for those who answer the calling, being a game designer is a labor of love.

I believe it's important to set realistic goals and expectations. I always encourage new designers to start small with modest goals and work up from there to more and more ambitious projects. I have seen new designers that start with something very ambitious and struggle with it. It is a discipline that will give back what you put in. The more games you design, the better you get at it.

So, start with a realistic goal and work to achieve it. You can always go big later. If you enjoy the whole process of creating games, then you'll keep creating them regardless of whether they get signed by a publisher. Then, it's only a matter of time before you'll have a game out in the world with your name on it.

## Asger Harding Granerud (*Flamme Rouge, 13 Days: The Cuban Missile Crisis*)

First, I just want to say I think this is a great angle for a book because there are a lot of people out there who have an idea for a game and they're not thinking about it as a product or how to get it published. Their primary goal is not to be published. There are a lot of people out there who approach it in that manner, so we've set up some game design networks here in Copenhagen specifically to help each other get published. This has worked out well for a lot of us here and not just me and Daniel (Skjold Pedersen).

When I started, I had been designing games for a long time where I'd been introducing house rules, creating further games or variants of chess, etc. I had been doing that for years and years when I eventually wanted to start designing my own games to try to get them published. So, I set myself a very simple goal. I picked a game and I restricted myself to one piece of paper for the rules. I could use both sides of the paper, but it must fit on that one piece of paper.

I think that's important if what you want to do is to become a game designer. And by game designer, I mean someone who has designed several games. Of course, you're also a game designer if you get one game signed, but you're not going to be able to call yourself a professional if you just do one big game and then don't do it ever again. That's not necessarily the goal for everyone and I'm not saying that one is better than the other, but the point is when you're starting out, you will be making more games and you will be keeping them focused. And those first games I made, they are never going to be published, and they're all crap.

But the point was that I wouldn't get stuck on that one single game. I made it, I moved onto the next one, I made the next one, and I moved on from that one. They weren't all great. Some of them would eventually be published. But by keeping them small, and giving yourself some constraints for rules or themes, you'll actually make sure that you can get through a project and finish a prototype that you get to a playtesting stage.

If you really want to get your game published, you have to realize that it's a numbers game. Even if you do all the right research and you think this publisher is really waiting for this kind of game and looking for it, because that's what they specialize in, maybe they've already signed a game like this that is coming out in the next 5 years. And you have no clue about this. You cannot pinpoint these things. It's more a shotgun perspective than a sniper perspective, especially when you're starting out. Daniel and I are now fairly well known, and we have met with these publishers many times before. In 2018, we held 26 meetings and pitched a total of 120 times during those 26 meetings.

So, it's a matter of getting used to a lot of no's and accepting that as a premise because you cannot predict the opposite. You cannot predict exactly what a publisher is looking for. So, make sure that they see your game. Even better, make sure that you have several games when you go into a publisher meeting because some of them will just tell you within 30 seconds of a pitch that they already signed that exact game or they stopped looking for it. And then you can start to show them all the games you have in your bag, which you didn't think would match them.

Maybe they have also made a change and they're going to start making family games within the next 2 years, which you wouldn't know about either. So maybe they are looking for these kinds of things as well. However, I'm not suggesting you pitch your second World War game to Haba.

Of course, you have to do a little basic research, but you shouldn't assume you know exactly what they're looking for. You should let them actually say "no" rather than just anticipate they will say no because there's no way to know for sure until you ask.

Asking a publisher what they're interested in and showing them you have other games leaves a better impression and can give you a long-lasting relationship with this publisher. They will take you more seriously if you can do this. If you have something else to show them, it may be of interest to them.

Your other game may not be far enough along for them to take a prototype, but they'll still see that you're working on it seriously.

So, if you really want to get a game published, don't just take one game to a meeting, take 10 games, and don't show them to one publisher, show them to 50 publishers and preferably shop them all around. You can start with your preferred five and then go to the next convention and show the next 10, etc.

I do think that if you want to get something published, at least here in Europe (I don't know about the US because I haven't done a lot of pitching in the US), I think that traveling to conventions is super important. It will become less important if you're lucky enough to get things published, because now you have a network with that publisher, and they will know that you're capable of working with them. Hopefully, they're happy with this and hopefully, you are happy with them. Then you can send games to this publisher in between conventions. But, for a new designer, going to a convention, shaking hands, and meeting publishers in person is at the top of the list of what I think you should be doing.

I would always suggest speaking to publishers in advance of Conventions. I've never done it the other way around where I just showed up at a publisher's booth. I think it's been fairly easy and in the first year, my partner got meetings set up within 2 days of emailing the publishers. I'm not saying that it's that easy all the time. But you have to remember that these publishers have staff at that convention that are there specifically looking at new prototypes. So, they're looking for you to come and show them these games. They are actually craving these meetings and by offering to show them your game, you're giving them something they want.

Now some of these publishers will ask for sell sheets and videos, etc. Do those as you please. The thing is, again, if you've got 10 games and you have to do detailed videos for all 10, then, in my opinion, you could probably sign 12 games instead of doing all these videos. So, I would much rather make sure that I write a very brief introduction and an email, then show up and actually pitch the game in person, because that first pitch is also better in person.

What I do is I write an email and then in the text I say, "Hey, we're coming to Spiel. We're printing prototypes and we would like to show you some games." We keep our emails short. We don't even write up what kinds of games they are. And then if we are bringing 5, 10, or 15 different prototypes, then maybe sometimes we will mention we have these three games that we think could be a fit for that specific publisher. We have more, but these three are the ones we would like to highlight.

Then we share a couple of sentences about each of these games, nothing more than that. Maybe I'm biased now and not used to how it is being unpublished because I can also now write at the top of my email that I'm the designer of three games and name them all, and the fact that they'll probably recognize that, of course, makes it easier. So, I'm not trying to say it is easy, but even back when we started out, we were just writing emails and asking for meetings. Publishers are there for that reason. They want those meetings.

As for the pitch itself, I know a lot of people are nervous about making this pitch and they think that they have to perform. Of course, that is true to an extent, but the way I say it to people and also how I tell it to myself is that no matter what I do in that meeting, no decision will be made there. The best case is that they will take a prototype and then that prototype would probably have to be played by the right people who are making those decisions. So, what you're actually pitching is for them to take home a prototype, but the actual selling of the game is something the game has to do on its own. That will be based on the work you have already put in, not what you say in that pitch meeting.

***Make sure to go to*** tinyurl.com/bgbonuspage ***to download all the bonuses and goodies mentioned in the book, including the 10 Minute Board Game Blueprint, sell sheet examples, pitch and email templates, the video that landed my first published game, plus a whole lot more.***

# References and Suggested Resources

Make sure to go to tinyurl.com/bgbonuspage to download all the bonuses and goodies mentioned in the book, including the 10-Minute Board Game Blueprint, sell sheet examples, pitch and email templates, the video that landed my first published game, plus a whole lot more.

## Books


Garfield, Richard and Steve Jackson. *Kobold Guide to Board Game Design*. Open Design LLC, 2011.

Koster, Raph. *Theory of Fun for Game Design*. O'Reilly Media, 2013.

Schell, Jesse. *The Art of Game Design: A Book of Lenses*. CRC PRESS, 2017.

Slack, Joe. *The Board Game Designer's Guide*. 2017.

Stegmaier, Jamey. *A Crowdfunder's Strategy Guide: Build a Better Business by Building Community*. Berrett-Koehler Publishers, 2015.

Tinsman, Brian, et al. *The Game Inventor's Guidebook*. Morgan James Publishing, 2008.

League of Game Makers Book Recommendations: http://www.leagueofgamemakers.com/a-game-designers-library-14-books-you-should-read/


## Blogs, Podcasts, & Websites


Board Game Design Lab—An excellent resource for information and my personal favorite podcast on game design: http://www.boardgamedesignlab.com/

Board Game Mechanics List: https://boardgamegeek.com/browse/boardgame mechanic

Boardgamegeek: www.boardgamegeek.com

Cardboard Edison—website and Compendium, a great source listing hundreds of publishers: http://cardboardedison.com/ http://cardboardedison.com/directoryinfo/

Component Studio (through the Game Crafter): https://component.studio/

Designing for Color Blindness: http://blog.usabilla.com/how-to-design-for-color-blindness/

Drive-Thru Cards: https://www.drivethrucards.com/

Game Crafter: https://www.thegamecrafter.com/

How to Become a Published Board Game Designer: https://gamedevelopment.tutsplus.com/articles/how-to-become-a-published-board-game-designer-cms-20815

Indie Game Alliance: https://www.indiegamealliance.com/
Inspiration to Publication (Bamboozle Brothers): https://inspirationtopublication.wordpress.com/the-steps-for-board-games/
Kickstarter Lessons and Amazing Self-publishing and Board Game Design Tips from Jamey Stegmaier of Stonemaier Games: https://stonemaiergames.com/kickstarter/how-to-design-a-tabletop-game/
Ludology http://ludology.libsyn.com/
Print and Play by Ad Magic https://www.printplaygames.com/
Printer Studio: https://www.printerstudio.com/
Tabletop Publishers: https://tabletoppublishers.com/

## Other Resources (Design Programs)

Canva: https://www.canva.com/
Inkscape: https://inkscape.org/en/
GIMP: https://www.gimp.org/

# Thank You!

Thank you so much for reading my book! There are tons of game design resources out there, so I'm very appreciative that you chose mine.

I'd really love to have your feedback and to know how my book was beneficial to getting your game one step closer to getting published.

**Please leave me a helpful REVIEW on Amazon.**

Help me spread the word so other designers can make and sign amazing games that we can all enjoy!

Thanks so much!

**~Joe Slack**

For Product Safety Concerns and Information please contact our EU representative GPSR@taylorandfrancis.com
Taylor & Francis Verlag GmbH, Kaufingerstraße 24, 80331 München, Germany

www.ingramcontent.com/pod-product-compliance
Ingram Content Group UK Ltd.
Pitfield, Milton Keynes, MK11 3LW, UK
UKHW021430080625
459435UK00011B/217

* 9 7 8 1 0 3 2 3 6 9 8 8 4 *